MANAGING CYBERSECURITY RISK

Edition 2 – 2018

Published by
Legend Business Books

Edited by
Jonathan Reuvid

Legend Business Ltd,
107-111 Fleet Street, London, EC4A 2AB
info@legend-paperbooks.co.uk | www.legendpress.co.uk

Contents © Legend Business, Jonathan Reuvid and Individual Contributors 2018
The right of the above authors to be identified as the authors of this work has been asserted in accordance with the
Copyright, Designs and Patents Act 1988. British Library Cataloguing in Publication Data available.

Print ISBN 9781787198913
Ebook ISBN 9781787198906
Set in Times. Printed by Opolgraf SA
Cover design by Simon Levy | www.simonlevyassociates.co.uk

Publishers Note
Every possible effort has been made to ensure that the information contained in this book is accurate at the time
of going to press, and the publishers and authors cannot accept responsibility for any errors or omissions, however
caused. No responsibility for loss or damage occasioned to any person acting, or refraining from action, as a result
of the material in this publication can be accepted by the editor, the publisher or any of the authors.

MANAGING CYBERSECURITY RISK

EDITION 2 – 2018

Published by Legend Business Books

Editor: Jonathan Reuvid, Legend Business Books

FOREWORD

I'm honoured to be invited to write the Foreword to this latest vital cyber security publication from Legend Business. In the Preface and four Sections to this publication, business leaders and technical practitioners will find great insights into the realities that business communities around the world are facing when they consider measures to improve their cyber resilience.

These are exciting and challenging times for any business connected to the Internet. For most of us, our business operations have become utterly dependent upon IT and communications systems to ensure that we deliver products and services to our customers.

In the early days of December 2017, as we publish this edition, we continue to see news of alleged Russian interference in elections. The UK's National Cyber Security Centre has warned Government Departments against using Russia-based technical security products in systems that have access to Government sensitive information – this is not new advice to anyone who has worked within Government security agencies. Nevertheless, publication of this threat, heralds an escalation in the online battle to protect our national and business systems against a long list of cyber threats.

In the US, several Senators have co-sponsored a Bill that, if passed, would see company executives facing up to 5 years in prison if they intentionally fail to report breaches within 30 days of discovery. A reaction no doubt to the latest Uber data breach scandal that saw the company admit that they had tried to cover-up a massive breach of customer and driver personal information. Compounded by their decision to negotiate a payment to the cyber criminals responsible, asking them to delete the stolen details of 57 million customers and drivers and to keep quiet about the successful breach.

Add to this, the ongoing use of social media to propagate terrorist radicalisation and its use to spread fake news and state-sponsored propaganda to hundreds of millions of users. Is it any wonder that business leaders are caught like rabbits in the headlights when they pause to consider how best to navigate and walk the tight-rope of successful execution of measures to cover cyber resilience, governance, compliance, regulation and legislation in this inter-connected world in which we operate.

As you read the articles in this edition, please consider at least one action for tomorrow – start by creating and implementing your very own cyber security strategy. One that seeks to ensure that you have set your business on a course to be the best it can be, in executing cyber protection measures. If you involve every member of staff in this venture, and you implement it with common sense measures it should become a "business as usual" part of every day business life.

Regardless of where you operate, I recommend you begin by looking at the UK's National Cyber Security Centre website at www.ncsc.gov.uk which is full of really great advice about how to protect your business from the vast majority of cyber threats.

John Lyons
Founder & Chairman of the International Cyber Security Protection Alliance and Chief Executive Officer, Cyber Essentials Direct – www.icspa.org and www.cyberessentialsdirect.com

PREFACE

In the cyber world, the last year has been marked by a further increase in the scale of crime and the ingenuity of criminals. Widespread publicity has attended spectacular attacks like Wannacry but the vast majority have been far from exotic and have succeeded simply because far too many users still behave as if an attack is something that happens to others but not to them.

This attitude is shortly going to become an even more expensive way of behaving than it is already. The regulators – in the form of the Information Commissioner – are coming after you. This volume spells out some of the potential consequences of the entry into force in May 2018 of GDPR and if you do not know what those initials stand for, it is imperative you read this volume. This legislation constitutes a major change in the rules governing the custody and use of personal third party data and lays out the financial penalties attached to breaches – which are swingeing. Faced with the possibility of a sizeable fine it is going to be important, as a means of mitigation, for "data controllers" to be able to show an auditable trail of the reasonable precautions that they put in place to prevent successful attack.

Currently, a UK Data Protection bill is going through Parliament which, among other things, fills in those parts of GDPR left to national discretion. It will also provide the basis for "equivalence" when this becomes needed on UK departure from the EU. The drafting leaves no doubt that the government takes the same stringent view as GDPR of the ownership rights of the individual over their data and the permissions needed for its use.

Having the ability to show the regulator the reasonable measures that have been taken to protect personal data means, of course, that these must have been put in place in the normal course of business management. It will not be possible to cook them up in the wake of an attack. There is much wise advice in this volume of both a technical nature – what the CISO and his team need to watch for and what they can do to reduce vulnerability to attack and of a management nature for the Board, the members of which can no longer get away with imagining that cyber is a subject that can be left to others. Resilience – the ability to recover from attack quickly – is increasingly, and rightly, being seen as a companion to security which, reasonable measures notwithstanding, cannot be guaranteed to be perfect. Against the eventuality of an attack senior management needs to have a rehearsed plan of action in place. The big losses, financial and reputational, tend to occur at the early stages of an attack when bewildered managers are trying to work out what is happening and what to do about it. Being alive to the changing threat picture is important and should be seen as part of the business environment about which managers should inform themselves. With the institution of the National Cyber Security Centre the government have taken a big step forward in making threat information more accessible.

Recently there have been an increasing number of attacks on the functioning of networks themselves, rather than on the data travelling on them. This is worrying especially as we now stand on the threshold of the fourth industrial revolution and we need to go beyond the current focus on personal data. A much greater level of consumer protection than exists at present for all types of data contained in devices attached to the internet is urgently needed. As one of the authors says, without real security and resilience of data and networks we will not be able to take advantage of the innumerable opportunities that the fourth industrial revolution is about to offer. And we shall be depriving ourselves of the sources of wealth that it will create.

When the government laid out the first cyber security strategy in 2010, it stated that it was intended to underpin the prosperity as well as the security of the UK. The Treasury was prepared to agree the expenditure precisely because of this. Since then, the focus has been on the prevention of losses. Increasingly we shall need to be alive to the importance of secure data of all kinds to the promotion of economic gain and wealth creation.

Rt Hon Baroness Pauline Neville-Jones

Former Minister of State for Security and Counter Terrorism

LIST OF CONTRIBUTORS

AlienVault® simplifies the way organisations detect and respond to today's evolving threat landscape. The company's unique and award-winning approach is used by thousands of customers and combines the multiple security controls of its all-in-one platform, AlienVault Unified Security Management, with the power of AlienVault's Open Threat Exchange®, the world's largest crowd-sourced threat intelligence community, to make effective and affordable threat detection attainable for resource constrained IT teams. AlienVault is a privately held company headquartered in Silicon Valley.

Mark Barmby is a thought leader who has worked on cyber related business challenges for over 10 years. He has been at PA Consulting Group since 2012 and specialises in working with defence and security organisations. Mark has a strong track record in driving operational improvement, leading high performance teams and delivering innovative cyber security solutions and results, drawing on his extensive military experience. He is a former senior military advisor who has a wealth of operational experience having been in the Royal Air Force for 23 years. In the last five years of his service, he led the conceptual and practical development of cyberspace in the military in both the UK and the US.

Kev Brear is the head of cyber resilience with the Grant Thornton UK LLP Cyber and Privacy Service's team. He has assisted in developing national and international standards on the subjects of resilience, crisis management and business continuity. He is currently a member of the BSI committee developing the new British standard on cyber risk and resilience. He holds an MSc from the University of Leicester in Risk, Crisis and Disaster Management and he is currently the course module leader for cyber resilience, at Cranfield University, for their Executive MBA programme.

Mike Carter and Amanda Price are Creative Directors at Layer 8 Ltd. The company specialises in the human factor in business security strategy and, since they started in 2014, Layer 8 has been working with organisations to raise employee awareness, change behaviours and develop security culture. Their belief is that, far from being the weakest link, employees are central to any cyber security solution – they have to be – and Layer 8's methods and approaches focus on people to harness their potential as frontline defenders of their organisation. Their products and services range from bespoke workshops, through ongoing "champions" campaigns to their communications suite, the Layer 8 Toolkit®. Today they are working with SMEs, FTSE100 and blue-chip companies, including organisations responsible for national infrastructure.

John Clelland is the Managing Director, founding partner and owner of Proteus-Cyber Ltd. He is an expert in the General Data Protection Regulation (GDPR), and the architect of Proteus GDPReady, a GDPR software product. John has been a guest speaker at numerous GDPR conferences, with extensive experience advising companies how to implement their GDPR program. John is also an expert in encryption and cyber security with over 30 years' experience architecting specialist IT/security systems.

Alexander Ellrodt is an experienced risk and resilience control manager with over 20 years' experience in the financial services industry. He has held numerous roles in business continuity, crisis management, fixed income control and human resources, all at large financial institutions in London and Frankfurt. Currently, Alexander is global head of IT Disaster Recovery at Deutsche Bank. In this function he is responsible for ensuring that regulatory and operational recovery risk controls are implemented and applied across the organisation including third party vendors. Alexander represents Deutsche Bank in various working groups and forums with the Bank of England and the European Central Bank. In this capacity, Alexander works closely with Information Security, IT Risk and Compliance. He holds a master's degree in Political Science from the University of Frankfurt and is a certified BCM (ISO 22301 & 27001) auditor. He has previously worked for a federal government agency as an aviation and diplomatic security officer.

Christopher Greany is a speaker and commentator on issues relating to financial crime and cyber threats. He is the Managing Director and Head of Group Investigations at Barclays. He is also responsible for the Barclays Global Insider Threat Programme and cyber forensics capability. Before joining the bank Christopher had a policing career spanning over 30 years. His last role was leading the UK and international policing response to Economic Crime and Cyber Protection as Commander in the City of London Police. Previously he led the National Police Coordination Centre, coordinating the UK policing response to national and international crisis and disaster.

Chris Greenslade is the Sales Director, founding partner and an owner of Proteus-Cyber Ltd. Passionate about customer satisfaction, Chris would like to discuss with you how Proteus®GDPReady™ could help your business move towards compliance with the GDPR.

Dan Hyde is a solicitor and partner at City law firm Penningtons Manches LLP. A pioneering cyber security lawyer, he identified cyberlaw as a distinct and developing area of law and put UK cyber security law on the map by writing the first professional reference book explaining what it was and how it could be applied to tackle the vast army of cyber threats and attacks. He has been instructed on a number of high profile cases and represents both corporates and individuals. An adviser to the Law Commission on cyber security legislation, Dan has lectured at esteemed institutions (University of London, Lloyds Underwriters and the Royal College of Surgeons) and is contributing editor of Modern Financial Regulation, a key professional reference work. His articles on cybercrime are published in the quality press and his commentaries broadcast on television and radio. The Legal 500 describes him as "calm under pressure", "skilled at managing the crossover between parallel civil and criminal proceeding" and "a lawyer of the highest calibre".

Nick Ioannou is an IT professional, author and blogger with over 20 years' corporate experience, including 15 years using cloud/hosted software as a service (SaaS) systems. He started blogging in 2012 on free software and IT tips (nick-ioannou.com), currently with more than 400 posts. His first book "Internet Security Fundamentals", currently available at www.booleanlogical.com, is an easy to under-stand guide to the most commonly faced security threats and criminal scams aimed at general users.

Karla Jobling is the founder of BeecherMadden, with nominations for a number of awards for entrepreneurship. She is also a judge for the Cyber Security Awards. Karla has over 10 years' experience recruiting within information security. She is passionate about encouraging more women into the cyber security industry and improving the diversity of the industry to help organisations build more successful teams. BeecherMadden recruits across the corporate governance sector, with offices in London, New York, Zurich and Singapore. While Karla specialises in senior appointments, BeecherMadden recruit from entry level upwards.

Richard Knowlton is Chairman of Richard Knowlton Associates, the security risk and resilience consultancy. He is a regular contributor to the media and at international conferences. Group Security Director of Vodafone 2009-2015, Richard worked earlier in Italy as Head of Security Global Operations with the UniCredit Group, the largest bank in Central and Eastern Europe. He is an honorary Life Member of the

International Security Management Association (ISMA), and a member of the Cyber Resilience Advisory Board of Digital Leaders.

Brian Lord OBE is Managing Director for PGI Cyber and previous Deputy Director for GCHQ, where he drove the modernisation programme across their most active technical operations and entire workforce. Brian oversaw both defensive and active cyber operations through an unparalleled experience of cyber threats, risks, opportunity and effective mitigation strategies. He is an eminent thought leader on cyber warfare and the intent and motivations across all cyber threat actions, and is regularly enlisted by media outlets as a cyber expert. Brian has built PGI's full spectrum of cyber security advice, technical service delivery and organisational/skill transformation for both public and private sector organisations.

Neill Newman is a seasoned information security professional with experience in governance, data protection, business continuity, information risk management, user awareness and incident management. He has designed and implemented strategic cyber resilience roadmaps across a variety of businesses and sectors, overseen by a number of UK, US and European regulators. Neill has operated at C-level and influenced numerous Boards over the years and is equally at home with high level business processes as well as low level technical change initiatives. He holds an MBA, a PhD in Electronic/Software Engineering and is interested in strategic issues for cyber risk management.

Richard Preece is a "hybrid" consultant and leader, who connects business and technical leadership so that they can maximise the opportunities and minimise the risks of the Digital Age; in particular, by taking an integrated approach to make organisations more agile and resilient. He is an Associate Director of Oakas; an Associate Lecturer for the Henley Business School GDPR Programme; a GCHQ Certified Trainer; and is an external Data Protection Officer (DPO) for several organisations. Due to his work, he is a co-opted core panel member of the new British Standard (BS31111:2018) Cyber Risk and Resilience – Guidance for Boards and Executive Management.

Vijay Rathour is a partner at Grant Thornton UK LLP where he is Head of the Digital Forensics Group. He has managed data breaches ranging from limited but highly sensitive losses of data by governmental agencies to the theft of over $100 million through intrusion and manipulation of SWIFT systems in a client bank. Vijay works at the interface of legal and technical teams, providing experience in strategic guidance and crisis management, regularly reporting to Boards and oversight committees. He is an ethical hacker and enjoys a role on the Committee of the Cybercrime Practitioners Association. He is also engaged by the Ministry of Justice to re-draft the Civil Procedure Rules on Electronic Disclosure and Investigative techniques for the modern era.

Jonathan Reuvid is the editor in chief and a partner of Legend Business Books Ltd. A graduate of the University of Oxford (MA, PPE) he embarked on a second career in publishing in 1989 after a career in industry, including the role of Director of European Operations of the manufacturing divisions of a Fortune 500 multinational and joint venture development in China. Jonathan has nearly 90 editions of more than 35 titles to his name as editor and part-author. He is a director of IPR Events London Ltd, an exhibition management company and President of the Community First Oxfordshire charity.

Nick Wilding is General Manager of Cyber Resilience at AXELOS Global Best Practice, a joint company set up in 2013 and co-owned by the UK Government and Capita plc, which owns and develops a number of best practice methodologies, including ITIL® and PRINC2®, used by organisations in more than 150 countries to enable them to work and operate more effectively. Nick is responsible for RESILIA™ Global Best Practice, a portfolio of cyber resilience best practice publications, certified training, staff awareness learning and leadership engagement tools designed to put the "human factor" at the centre of cyber resilience strategy, enabling effective recognition, response to and recovery from cyber attacks.

RESILIA™ FRONTLINE

EFFECTIVE CYBER SECURITY AWARENESS TRAINING FOR ALL YOUR EMPLOYEES

Ensuring your most **valuable and precious information** remains secure from cyber-attacks is now a critical priority for every organization. But your cyber security is only as good as the attitudes and behaviours of *your people*.

RESILIA™ Frontline cyber security awareness training gives your employees, the **simple, practical guidance** they need to make the right decisions at the right time.

Key features:

- Short, engaging, relevant and regular online cyber security awareness training

- 10 subject areas across four learning pathways: Managing Online Risk, Keeping Safe Online, Protecting Information and Safe Device Use

- Written and designed by international cyber security and learning and development specialists

- Measure, learn and adapt via a comprehensive management information suite

- GCHQ Certified Training (GCT) Provider.

Make your people your greatest defence against cyber-attacks today!

Visit AXELOS.com/resilia-frontline to find out more and request a live demonstration of RESILIA Frontline.

Alternatively, to speak to someone in the team and arrange a free 14-day trial, please contact resilia.frontline@axelos.com.

**Proteus®
GDPReady™**

Proteus-Cyber are specialists in the General Data Protection Regulation. Our software can run in the cloud or on-premises.

- **Fastest route to GDPR compliance**
- **First reports within four weeks**
- **Aim to be compliant within 6 months**
- **Demonstrate compliance easily**
- **Most comprehensive tool (Including off-the-shelf tools**
  - consent rules, SARs, breach notification, etc

Subject Access

Privacy impact

Easy to use

**One-Stop GDPR Software Solution
Proteus®GDPReady™
www.proteuscyber.com**

Low co

Personal data

Legal framework

**Contact us today about using GDPReady
sales@proteuscyber.com**

- **Simple surveys to build Data Register**
- **Full Privacy Impact Assessment (PIA/DPIA)**
- **Consent engine**
- **Easy reporting (e.g. Article 30 report)**
- **Subject Access Requests**

- **3rd party processor assessmen**
- **Breach notification (Article 33)**
- **GDPR awareness training**
- **Multilingual**
- **Lawfulness of processing**

In a Complex, Dynamic and Uncertain World

Join the Dots to Make Your Company More Anticipatory and Resilient

Gain Insights to Support Effective Governance and Risk Management

To prosper in the Digital Age, requires

anticipation, agility and resilience. Oakas works

with NATO, Governments and commercial

companies, to help them prosper and survive.

Providing the means to develop understanding of

the opportunities and threats they are facing and

how to achieve their strategy.

OAKAS ORGANISATIONAL RESILIENCE

Learn more at www.oakas.co.uk

Legend 📖 Press

Who are we?

Legend press was founded in 2005 and is focused primarily on publishing literary fiction, crime thrillers, women's fiction, historical fiction, and young adult novels.

Visit our website for information on events and new releases as well as blog posts from authors and details on how to send your manuscript to our submissions department: www.legendtimesgroup.co.uk/legend-press

Passionate about books?

The Legend 100 club is a group of bloggers and reviewers who hear about our upcoming titles, receive free ebooks ahead of publication and post reviews on blogs, Amazon, Goodreads, netgalley and other literary publications.

If you'd like to join or find out more about becoming a Legend 100 reviewer, get in touch at imogenharris@legend-paperbooks.co.uk.

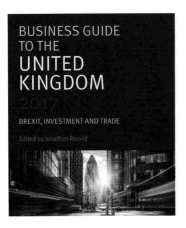

Published: 30 September 2017
ISBN (Paperback): 9781785079139
ISBN (Ebook): 9781785079122
Rights: World

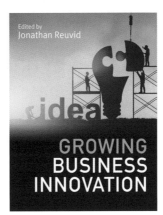

Published: 31st October 2017
ISBN (Paperback):
9781787198937 ISBN (Ebook):
9781787198920
Rights: World

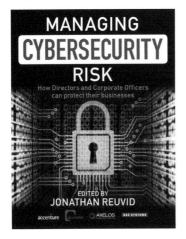

Published: 30 November 2016
ISBN (Paperback): 9781785079153
ISBN (Ebook): 9781785079146
Rights: World

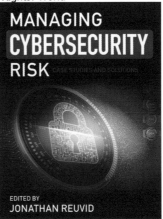

Published: 30 November 2017
ISBN (Paperback): 9781787198913
ISBN (Ebook): 9781787198906
Rights: World

Published: 30 April 2016
ISBN (Paperback): 9781785079320
ISBN (Ebook): 9781785079337
Rights: World

Published: 28 May 2011
ISBN (Paperback): 9781907756382
ISBN (Ebook): 9781908248169
Rights: World

GREAT LEADERS
PRIORITISE INNOVATION

66% of organisations will not survive without innovation, yet only **24**% have the skills to succeed.

HOW DO YOU COMPARE?

Take our online assessment:

paconsulting.com/innovation-assessment

Every day, our consultants, designers and technologists use innovative approaches to deliver amazing results.

Make the Difference.

INTRODUCTION

The first edition of Managing Cybersecurity Risk, published a year ago, was intended as a wake-up call to the directors and senior management of SMEs and all those larger companies that had not recognized their vulnerability to cyber attack or had not taken appropriate action to address cyber risk.

This second edition takes the discussion a stage further with a focus on the human factor and training and a section of the book devoted to the implications for cybersecurity of General Data Protection Regulation (GDPR). Responsibility for cyber infringement policy and process remain firmly with the Board. AXELOS Resilia, the thought leader in cyber education and a content partner, identifies storytelling as an effective tool in cyber learning and has contributed a series of a cautionary tales for the final part of the book.

As I noted in my introduction to the previous edition, selection of a managed service provider (MSP) with the most appropriate software for your business is a challenge, particularly for those of us who are IT unskilled. We have searched among those MSPs whose offerings are comprehensible to the layperson and whose products appear both cost effective and affordable and have chosen California-based AlienVault as our content partner for the book. The four chapters on intrusion detection, ransomware and incident response were provided by the AlienVault team. In 2017 AlienVault received an average rating of 8 out of 10 from TrustRadius, the highly rated review site for business technology serving both buyers and vendors.

Among the other contributors who are leading specialists in their fields, are cybersecurity practitioners with international experience in banking, mobile telephony, the law, accountancy, IT, recruitment and a range of management consultancy. To each of these authors I offer my sincere thanks for sharing their expertise and to John Lyons and to Pauline Neville-Jones my appreciation for their respective Foreword and Preface.

Already, we are planning for the next edition of Managing Cybersecurity Risk to be published in a year's time. One new topic which is certain to feature will be the growing impact of AI and Cybersecurity on each other.

Jonathan Reuvid
Editor

Part One

Cybersecurity in the Information Age

1.1 BUILDING BUSINESS RESILIENCE

Nick Wilding, AXELOS RESILIA

INTRODUCTION

This chapter contends that a missing key in the creation and growth of a truly cyberresilient organisational culture lies in building a vigilant and resilient workforce through effective awareness learning for all.

KEYWORDS are: cyber security, cyber resilience, resilient workforce, storytelling, boardroom engagement.

THE NATURE OF THE CHALLENGE

Baroness Dido Harding, the outgoing CEO of TalkTalk, called cybercrime 'the crime of our generation' when she was thrust into the media gaze following their high-profile breach in October 2015. Her experience is by no means unique — the threat we all face is real and relentless.

Symantec, in their 'Internet Security Threat Report' published in April 2016, noted that they had:

'...*discovered more than 430 million unique new pieces of malware in 2015, up 36 percent from the year before. Perhaps what is most remarkable is that these numbers no longer surprise us. As real life and online become indistinguishable from each other, cybercrime has become a part of our daily lives. Attacks against businesses and nations hit the headlines with such regularity that we've become numb to the sheer volume and acceleration of cyber threats.'*[1]

---

1. Symantec (April 2016), 'Internet Security Threat Report', available at https://www.symantec.com/ content/dam/ symantec/docs/reports/istr-21- 2016-en.pdf (accessed 26th July, 2017).

This 'numbness' is echoed in research carried out by the National Institute of Standards and Technology (NIST)[2] in the US. They assessed perceptions and beliefs about cybersecurity and online privacy, and identified that people are increasingly desensitised to constant reminders about cyber risks. One of the research respondents, an 'average technology user', commented:

'I don't pay any attention to those things any more ... people get weary of being bombarded by "watch out for this or watch out for that".'

SECURITY FATIGUE

The last quote highlights the difficulties we face in moving beyond the frustration, weariness and 'security fatigue' many of us feel from the bombardment of messages about the dangers lurking online.

The NIST research found that many of us often feel out of control or resigned to doing nothing about online security. Now, take these attitudes into the workplace and organisations are faced with a real dilemma. The reality is that cyber attackers often find it easier to communicate with, engage and influence the behaviours of our staff than we do. Technology is not the only answer — just a part of it. In 2015, Tom Farley, President of the New York Stock Exchange, said in his introduction to 'Navigating the Digital Age: The Definitive Cybersecurity Guide for Directors and Officers':

'It is important companies remain vigilant, taking steps to proactively and intelligently address cybersecurity risks within their organisations. Beyond the technological solutions developed to defend and combat breaches, we can accomplish even more through better training, awareness and insight into human behaviour. Confidence, after all, is not a measure of technological systems, but of the people who are entrusted to manage them.'

THE HUMAN FACTOR

But there's a huge challenge here — one which was starkly highlighted in Verizon's 2015 Data Breach Investigations Report:[3] the great majority — estimated to be 90 per cent — of successful cyberattacks succeed because of *human error*. That means

---

2. NIST, available at https://www.nist. gov/news-events/news/2016/10/

security-fatigue-can-cause-computer-users-feel- hopeless-and-act-recklessly (accessed 27th July, 2017).

3. Center for Internet Security, available at http:// www.verizonenterprise.com/resources/reports/ rp_data-breach-investigation-report_2015_en_xg.pdf (accessed 26th July, 2017).

anyone in any organisation, irrespective of their role or seniority, can enable an attack to succeed through their unwitting actions. Jim Baines, the apocryphal CEO whom I cite in Chapter 5.1, couldn't agree more:

'Unwitting is the point. Some of my friends say "witless" but that's another matter. The point is, we were complacent. We thought it was a technical not a human issue. But it's all about the human.'

Because most organisations don't think this way, the cyber attackers will always have the upper hand. They only need to be successful once in their relentless targeting of our human vulnerabilities, whereas we must maintain constant vigilance. In Jim's case, he was sent an email purporting to be from someone he'd met at a corporate golf event. The email offered pictures of his achievements on the fairway. He opened it on his business laptop and thought nothing of it. The names used were all familiar; one was from his distant past. It all seemed to make sense. But the attachment contained malware that infected the systems of Baines Packaging. Jim happened to be putting together a presentation for one of his major clients, a huge food conglomerate, and he put the presentation on a flash drive, went to a meeting and handed it to his contact — an old friend — who then infected that company's systems. A chain reaction began. Jim's entire livelihood was compromised.

That chain of events powerfully illustrates why we all — from the boardroom to the engine room and beyond — have a specific role to play in protecting our most precious information and assets. If an organisation's people represent its greatest vulnerability, then it follows they can also be its most important and cost-effective defence against attacks. I would suggest that we're at a crossroads in our collective corporate response to the cyber risks we all face: one where many will continue to invest in more technology and expect that multiple layers of technical defence will suffice. Another group – the market leaders, pioneers and innovators, but increasingly the 'just plain sensible' – will change direction and embrace an enterprise-wide approach, led from the top, which uses new methods to engage and openly reward good cyber behaviours, from top to bottom.

On the road taken by this group, storytelling and the business language used will play a vital role in an adaptive and open approach to learning. It's these firms that also understand that cyber resilience will become a key market differentiator for asserting competitive advantage as customers, partners and — let us not forget — regulators (particularly with the General Data Protection Regulation [GDPR] coming into effect in March 2018) increasingly demand demonstrable proof that their most precious information is being kept safe and secure.

Many firms also increasingly understand that their cyber risks need to be managed in balance with the immense opportunities for operational transformation, innovation and efficiency that digital technologies now offer. As Daniel Dobrygowski, the

Global Leadership Fellow for the IT industry at the World Economic Forum, said in January 2017:

'Cyber risk is a systemic challenge and cyber resilience is a public good. Without security and resilience in our networks, it will be impossible to safely take advantage of the innumerable opportunities that the Fourth Industrial Revolution is poised to offer. Responsible and innovative leaders, therefore, are seeking ways to deal with these risks.'[4]

Storytelling plays an important role in responding to this systemic challenge; stories spark emotions, and they help people to remember information.

YOUR STRONGEST DEFENCE

Mostly, cybersecurity is communicated within organisations as a set of statistics and data about the latest threats, the changing techniques adopted by cyber attackers and the number of events and incidents experienced. As a method of bringing about systemic and cultural change, this is a flawed approach.

I believe that the opportunity is clear: staff are not, as is so often lazily reported, 'our weakest link'. They are instead our most powerful and effective defence against attacks and only as 'weak' as the strength of the awareness training we give them. But does this training engage? Is it relevant and relatable to the learner? Does it provide simple, practical guidance? Is it focused on giving them the confidence to change their existing behaviours and to discuss incidents with their colleagues? Does it tell a strong story about what 'good' looks like?

The sad truth is that most organisations continue to educate their people with an annual information security awareness e-learning exercise. It can take over an hour to complete and typically ignores some basic rules for effective learning. With cyber attacks relentlessly targeting and threatening our most sensitive and valuable information, forgetting, sadly, is no longer an option. Ignorance isn't a defence anymore. The risks and potential impacts are too great.

In this vital area of staff training and development, one size doesn't fit all. The current 'all staff, once a year' approach simply does not influence or sustain long-term behavioural change. At best, it reminds us of some essentials; at worst, it's treated as a necessary evil, a distraction, and something to be completed as quickly as possible.

Annual e-learning will not instil and sustain the cyber-resilient behaviours that employees need today. We're trying to 'programme' our people in the same way we

---

4. Dobrygowski, D. (January 2017), 'Why being a responsible leader means being cyber-resistant', available at https://www.weforum.org/ agenda/2017/01/why-being-a-responsible-leader- means-being-cyber-resilient/ (accessed 26th July, 2017).

programme computers: to do certain things, in defined ways, at certain times. This approach doesn't work with human beings.

During January 2016, AXELOS RESILIA, with IPSOS Mori[5] carried out research among those responsible for information security awareness learning in their organisations. We wanted to find out how well prepared members of the UK's workforce were for a cyber attack in the companies they work for. The results were sobering.

While it was positive to note that 99 per cent of business executives responsible for cyber awareness learning said that information security awareness learning was 'important to minimise the risk of security breaches', less than a third (28 per cent) judged their organisation's cybersecurity awareness learning as 'very effective' at changing staff behaviour.

A similar minority (32 per cent) were 'very confident' that the learning was relevant to their staff, while 62 per cent were only 'fairly confident'. This comparatively low level of corporate confidence in the ability of people to deal with a cyber attack is simply not good enough in an era where cybercrime has become 'business as usual'. It reflects either a lack of understanding or a state of denial about the impact that a successful cyber attack can have on a business.

Organisations cannot continue to accept this low level of employee awareness and competence in the face of sophisticated cybercriminals who are constantly adapting their methods. Imagine how your customers would respond if told, 'We're *fairly confident* that your confidential information is safe from attack'. Equally, a report to a board of directors that the level of confidence in the organisation's information security awareness is only 'fair' would provoke some serious alarm. If company boards are not asking questions about the current effectiveness of their awareness learning programme and what is being done to improve their organisational cyber resilience, then they should be. Now!

AWARENESS TRAINING

What determines the capability and performance of employees is the relevance and effectiveness of the training they're provided with and the behaviours they adopt as a result.

What needs to be understood is that we all learn differently and at different speeds. We need to offer awareness training that provides our people with multiple approaches that appeal to the widest possible spectrum. This way, they are far more likely to have the confidence to share and discuss experiences, to get proactively involved

---

5. AXELOS (April 2016), 'UK organizations' cyber security awareness learning needs to enter the 21st century', available at https://www.axelos.com/news/ uk-organization-cyber-awareness-needs-to-enter-21c (accessed 26th July, 2017).

in their own learning, to champion resilience to others and to continuously learn and adapt. That's why the picture painted by our research suggests that the current annual compliance-based approach, which is still relied upon by most organisations, is failing.

The same challenges are being faced in the boardroom. The impact of a major attack can be catastrophic and the boards of many high-profile global brands have already felt the reputational and financial damage that can ensue. Many more continue to struggle to properly understand what they can do to address this and what good cyber resilience looks like for them.

THE BOARDROOM CHALLENGE

While business leaders and senior executives strive to mitigate and respond more effectively to their cyber risks, the challenge remains a big one for boards. The UK Government's annual FTS 350 Cyber Governance Health Check research published in May 2016 [6] pinpoints many of the problems faced in the boardroom. The research, carried out with CEOs and CFOs, highlighted that:

- Only 33 per cent of boards have clearly set out and understood their appetite for cyber risk.

- Only 16 per cent have a very clear understanding of where the company's key information assets are shared with third parties.

- Over 50 per cent said: 'We listen occasionally — e.g. a bi-annual update, plus being told when something has gone wrong' in answer to the question: 'Which of the following statements best describes how cyber risk is handled in your board governance process?'

- Over 60 per cent have either not at all or only loosely defined their appetite for cyber risk, both for existing business and for new digital innovations.

In all too many boardrooms their organisation's resilience to cyber risks does not form a key part of the agenda. They remain largely 'blindsided' to the nature and impact of the risks they face and are not communicating in an informed and effective 'tone from the top' to all their people.

Consequently, many will continue to 'sleepwalk' into reacting to a crisis rather than taking adequate precautions to mitigate their risks before a crisis occurs. Personal and

---

6. GOV.UK. 'Cyber Governance Health Check 2015/16 available at https://www.gov.uk/goverment/publications/ cyber-governance-health-check-2015/26 (accessed 26th July 2017)

corporate reputations have been irreparably damaged as a result. In the digital age, five seconds is perhaps more accurate.

Just as our technical security controls must constantly evolve and adapt to combat changing cyber threats and vulnerabilities, so we need to ensure all our people maintain their awareness learning and are provided with the appropriate, practical guidance on a continual basis that fits the needs and requirements of the organisation.

If you would like to find out more, you can contact Nick Wilding at nick.wilding@axelos.com

1.2 ENTERPRISE SCALE VULNERABILITY SCANNING

Dr. Neill Newman – Retail Money Market Ltd

THE BEGINNING

A number of years ago I was leading the cyber team for a medium sized organisation with a very large technology footprint, heavily regulated in multiple jurisdictions around the globe, audited to death....

My team and I had always planned to roll out internal vulnerability scanning to identify and measure what we believed were the weakest points in our processes – poor patching and configuration management. However, whenever we scoped the problem the costs/timescales looked daunting.

One day we had a visit from our regulator, who brought along their cyber assessment team; our internal 2nd line risk management team also joined us. We were grilled for hours on how we were undertaking various cyber activities, a completely holistic view, then the focus of attention turned to vulnerability scanning.

External scanning was fine, systems were in place, reports generated, issues risk assessed and prioritised for remediation. "What about internal scanning?" the regulator asked. I replied that it was something we had considered, however there were no internal scanning projects at this point in time.

INTERNAL VULNERABILITY SCANNING IS NOT EASY

A few days later our 2nd line risk management team visited us again, and asked, "If you already have external vulnerability scanning, surely it's easy to switch it on internally?"

While I liked our risk guys, they obviously had no idea of the monumental complexity of this request in an organisation such as ours. Then the icing on the cake:

"Can we get this in place in six months so when the regulator comes back we can say it's complete?"

I composed myself and replied that we would look into it and provide detailed plans with timescales/costs.

My team and I had a very open meritocratic communication style, with some of the best engineers I could wish for, who were highly experienced, motivated and vociferous in a positive way. After relaying the desire of our 2nd line guys, and after they had shared their feelings on how absurd the request was, I asked them one question. What would it take to identify everything on our network, on an ongoing basis, as close to real time as possible?

I knew my team liked a challenge, their eyes lit up. "What about costs/resources?" they asked. "Ignore that for now, start with the basics, do it well. Tell me what it would take." was my reply. Within a few days we had a plan.

ENTERPRISE NETWORKS ARE BIG AND SCARY

To put our enterprise network into context, we had 10 data centres across the globe (US, Asia, EU), end users in 30 countries, approximately 4,000 /24 subnets, and multiple owners, administrators and legal/regulated entities all controlling access to the network.

While this is not huge compared to the likes of Amazon or eBay, it is still a world away from a small office network.

Our review of vendors' enterprise vulnerability scanners had left us underwhelmed. They often talked about "simple" processes to "identify, analyse, mitigate and manage" vulnerabilities. Both commercial and open source vulnerability scanners appeared to believe you could see all devices on the network and have perfect asset databases with nice neat network segregation.

These assumptions around "lab" conditions, where all variables are known and under control, is far from most enterprises' experience, and our organisation was no exception. In practice it is not easy to identify <u>everything</u> on your network using off-the-shelf offerings.

Enterprise networks are often developed in an evolutionary style and what starts off as a nice neat design is adapted in a piecemeal fashion over years/decades. Legacy constraints and mission critical environments often mean it is difficult to get complete control of the enterprise networks. Organisational acquisitions exacerbate this issue, and can lead to unintended network segregation, overlapping subnet ranges with internal firewalls all over the place, not to mention a plethora of weird and exotic devices all live on the network, waiting for a cunning individual to exploit the vulnerability you were unaware of.

The complexities our organisation faced meant that the approaches to vulnerability scanning that most vendors try to implement were not effective on our network, and in some cases not even feasible.

HOW TO SKIN THE ELEPHANT IN THE ROOM

We needed to identify every endpoint on our network to seed the vulnerability scanner. This centralised network device repository took a few weeks to develop, but took many months of testing before we could rely on the results.

The heart of the system involved read-only access to all network devices, all switches, routers, firewalls, load balancers, both physical and virtual. We automatically enumerated and extracted all arp tables, IP addresses, physical ports and routing tables on all devices, and these were stored centrally. The enumeration ran automatically every 15 minutes so we had a snapshot of all devices on our network within that time period.

The data obtained enabled other health checks to be performed. The routing tables and gateways identified were compared against the list of "known" network devices from the networks team. We already had a SIEM with firewall logs and the list of identified IP addresses were matched against this to identify devices on our network which were not sending logs. Internal DNS quality was assessed by matching forward and reverse zones against the list of identified IP addresses. Lastly, the data quality of the asset databases was determined by matching against the list of known devices.

We produced a daily data quality report with KPIs showing the number of devices identified in each region/entity, the number of devices not sending logs to the SIEM, the number of devices not in DNS and the number of devices not in the asset databases.

NOTHING GOES SMOOTHLY

Despite months of testing, we encountered a number of problems along the way:

- Initially we had overlooked the use of DHCP on our desktop subnets so we looked to obtain the DHCP logs and store these with appropriate timestamps.

- As previously stated, we had about 4,000 /24 subnets. This was identified by enumerating all of the network devices; however, the networks teams were only aware of approximately half of those in use.

- Out of a possible 1 million internal IP addresses we identified approximately 45,000 devices actually plugged into the network, which was more than anybody had realised.

- We identified a small data centre in Asia Pacific that nobody knew about (an old acquisition where the people with the appropriate knowledge had left).

- The daily data quality reports showed that most asset databases were very poorly managed, with typically less than 20% of devices being recorded.

- Internal DNS was hit and miss – forward lookups were reasonable, but reverse lookups were almost non-existent.

The key requirement for internal vulnerability scanning is an accurate asset database and DNS. Network based vulnerability scanners (as well as forensic devices and IDS systems) will usually only look at IP addresses. If you have no way of looking up an IP address in DNS, no record in an asset database, and no record of what devices are plugged into your network, how are you going to investigate and rectify any vulnerabilities found?

INTERNAL DNS AND ASSET DATABASES – IGNORE AT YOUR PERIL

The asset databases within our organisation needed a significant amount of work. Details of technical and business owners of each asset were needed so vulnerability statuses could be communicated and findings remediated.

However, the asset databases needed to contain much more than just a machine name/IP address/owner. Decisions were needed for how to document multiple physical interfaces with a single IP address, multiple IP addresses per physical interface and multiple interfaces per machine and virtual interfaces. We also had to make decisions on how to store "other" equipment such as phones, photo copiers, wireless access points etc. and then how the internal DNS should handle the above.

At this point, hopefully, the reader will start to appreciate the complexity of the problem. This "simple" internal vulnerability scanning challenge uncovered a secret that exists in most IT organisations, that most enterprises do not know what assets are on their network or who owns them.

START YOUR ENGINES

We explained to our 2nd line and senior management that internal vulnerability scanning was a journey and we could not provide a concrete date by when it would be complete. We had supporting evidence to show the complexity of the problem and how we were going to tackle it. Thankfully senior management trusted our judgement and allowed us to continue.

Once the politics were out of the way, work began in earnest. We determined the change/scanning windows with critical systems owners (at least these were known). Test scans produced rough scan timings; however, we found that each machine, environment, and physical location produced varying results at different times of the day. From this data we estimated how long it would take to scan the entire enterprise based on the average scan time multiplied by the number of devices.

Further issues were identified during this testing phase – firewalls blocking our scans, both host and network based. Whitelisting the scanning machines was not as easy as it sounds. Identifying who owned the network firewalls was easy, but host based firewalls were harder to update due to poor asset database information and the difficulty in tracking down owners.

The test scans also highlighted a number of problems with our scanning architecture:

- There were unrouteable networks from the initial scanning locations so multiple scanning nodes were needed.

- Multiple virtual machines inside physical chassis presented problems – virtual scanning nodes attached to internal VLANs which could see all virtual machines were needed.

- Slow network links to the furthest reaches of our enterprise network meant we had to deploy local scanning nodes at certain locations around the globe.

- For some large locations a single scanning node could not scan all the devices in an appropriate timescale, so multiple scanning nodes were needed.

This architecture was unique to our infrastructure, not because *we* were unique, but because all organisations networks are. This is one of the reasons why off-the-shelf vendor solutions cannot easily be dropped into an enterprise environment and expected to work.

RIP THE ENGINE OUT AND START AGAIN

Our final architecture implemented, we distributed vulnerability scanning nodes with a central management point to control the nodes and to collate the results. This architecture allowed for both organic and step change growth (e.g. when senior management buys another company, which happened to us several times).

However, a distributed scanning architecture comes at a cost. Whether you choose physical devices or virtual appliances the only real area for cost control is with the scanning node license fees. For large enterprise environments the usual licensing models are cost prohibitive. We were lucky as we had negotiated an unlimited license for the vulnerability scanner (infinite IPs and scanning engines).

We did look at using open source scanning nodes combined with commercial vulnerability feeds, as on paper there could have been significant costs savings. However, we believed the development/integration costs would have outweighed any savings due to the need for skilled people to engineer and maintain the solution.

IT'S ALIVE...

As mentioned previously, the vulnerability scanner could not work in isolation of other key processes and considerations.

- Integration with the central network device identification repository to allow automatic time-based suppressions with our operations centre would have been ideal. While we never got that far we were aware that we could have flooded the SOC with alerts if we had not put in blanket suppressions.

- Automatic report integration with the asset databases was also desirable to distribute scanning results. We had no intention of manually sifting through a vulnerability report of 45,000 devices to send to multiple owners; however, this needed the appropriate asset data in order to send the correct report to the appropriate owner.

- We were careful to avoid integration with a ticketing system. While the idea of automatically raising a ticket for every vulnerability identified would have keep the auditors happy, we decided this should only be undertaken after the scanning environment had been tested thoroughly.

- Scheduling and risk assessment were another important area. Blindly switching on a scanner and hoping for the best could have caused havoc. Vulnerability Scanning can cause instability, therefore we opted for appropriate testing on non-critical devices/environments first. Before scanning any production environments, we identified, discussed and agreed an appropriate scanning windows with the asset owners.

Consideration was also given to the worst-case scenario, when it all goes wrong and a scanning node goes rogue, resulting in service-affecting incidents. We could not be in a position where the vendor's software was not doing as we asked, so we spent time thinking about how to forcibly prevent scans overrunning past their allotted scanning window. We solved this problem by placing time based ACLs on the network switches. These could be manually enabled, blocking any traffic coming from our scanning sensors. We never had to use them but we slept at night knowing we had control should this situation arise.

We also steered away from using the pretty vendor GUIs for managing and scheduling scans as they did not scale well for our enterprise. Instead, we used dedicated job/batch schedulers to control the automation. The same was true for gathering the results and processing the data. We stored scanning results in an SQL database as it was easier to manipulate large data sets and to produce the customised reporting we required.

WE HAVE THE RESULTS, NOW WHAT?

Misunderstanding the reports was something we often had to deal with, the most common discussions occurring when a severity vulnerability rating and a risk rating were confused. Just because a severe vulnerability occurs on a restricted test platform does not mean it has the same risk profile as if the same severe vulnerability occurred on an Internet facing platform.

A lot of time was spent educating those reading the reports so they did not jump to conclusions. Pareto analysis was also used to prioritise the effort/risk return, as we often had so much information it was impossible to address all issues in a timely manner. On occasion, a single missing patch applied across the entire estate would address a large number of vulnerabilities quickly.

The initial reports came as a shock to senior management as their understanding of the environment was wide of the mark. Having hard data to base decisions on assisted in influencing and prioritising remediation efforts. Also, having a complete view of what devices were plugged into the network assisted us in demonstrating that some vendors' management tools were only looking at 30-40% of the actual technology footprint on the network.

NO BLANK CHEQUES

Some will say that the scale of the problem we were trying to address was too big and that it should have been broken down into more manageable pieces, focused around critical services. While I understand the rationale behind this thinking, I am reminded of the infamous Donald Rumsfeld phrase: "the unknown unknowns". It is not usually the things you know about which will bite you, but those things you were unaware of. Sun Tzu summed this up: "If you know neither the enemy nor yourself you will be imperilled in every battle". While I have some sympathy for those who take the piecemeal method, I believe it is conveniently or unwittingly ignoring the unknowns and therefore the riskier approach.

I have been asked a number of times what it took to perform this seemingly mammoth task – many assume lots of money and an army of staff. It took a small, technically experienced, dedicated security team who were passionate about securing the environment, who were 100% committed to the goal over many years and who were left to get on with solving the problem rather than getting bogged down in organisational politics/bureaucracy. It took supportive management who shared the goal without pressures to deliver, and it also needed a networks team who understood how the whole enterprise hung together and were willing to working alongside a security team who were pushing the boundaries.

A significant amount of trial and error occurred over the years. I have skipped over many things and timescales have been compressed in order to fit this journey into a few pages. It took lots and lots of time, really, lots, years. Would I do it again? Absolutely…

1.3 CYBECRIME – TRANSLATING THE TECH FROM THE FLOOR TO THE BOARDOOM

Christopher Greany, Barclays Bank Group Investigations and Insider Threat Program

Jeremy Fleming, the head of GCHQ, recently said, "If GCHQ is to continue to help keep the country safe, then protecting the digital homeland — keeping our citizens safe and free online – must become and remain as much part of our mission as our global intelligence reach and our round-the-clock efforts against terrorism."

His words are timely, and tell us how serious the cybercrime threat is today. GCHQ, who monitor threats from outside the UK, are not known for their public facing side and commentary on cybercrime is more commonly heard from the National Cyber Security Centre, itself closely affiliated to GCHQ.

Fleming's words are also telling in that he spoke of a "digital democracy, almost" where the liberty of citizens must be protected whilst dealing with the criminality that is sadly inherent within the internet.

I have long spoken before about how devastating a cyber attack can be, similar to terrorism. It doesn't have the immediacy and shocking visual nature of conventional terrorism or other crime in the physical sense and in many ways this is why there appears to be a struggle within people and companies in investing more in cyber security and cyber prevention.

Going back to the IRA bombing of the Grand Hotel Brighton in 1984, the terrorists said, " We only have to be lucky once, you have to be lucky always." Nothing has changed in this respect and when it comes to cybercrime there is an air of inevitability around this too.

There is also confusion, especially for smaller companies, on what to do, where to spend the precious money they may have to spare and who to trust in an increasingly tech-speak-heavy and buoyant cyber market place. Many promise the silver bullet, the fix-it-all-in-one, and everyone has the latest product, better than the other competitors. And this is the problem, the language is confusing, especially at board level, and many boards are not used to it and feel they can't ask the questions they feel more comfortable with. Contrast, for example, when a large or small corporation relocates to new offices. Board members become experts on architecture, soft furnishings, sofa and desk design – they are comfortable asking the questions, unlike when the cyber expert talks about implementing DMARC to prevent phishing, or the latest cyber attacks as a result of social engineering. Nervousness sets in and critical business risk discussions in the C suite become an "IT issue".

Language is key, and in many ways the word 'cyber' has helped caused some of the confusion. It has a science fiction ring to it, when in fact it became commonplace in the 1940s as part of cybernetics, the link between engineering, humans and machines. Go back further and it was used in a different form by the Greeks, all, of course, before the modern computer was invented.

In reality we are talking about computer networks, which are usually linked on the Internet or World Wide Web. It's that simple – humans doing things through the use of linked computers, whether they be traditional computers we are used to seeing or computers that control other machines, payment systems or anything else. I have never seen a computer arrested, it is humans using computers just like armed criminals use guns to attack their victims; it is just a tool to commit crime, albeit on an industrial scale.

The tech speak also confuses people, and whilst that is good for the techies who speak the language, it is not so good for the CEOs or the COOs or just the general public. Often because of the language barriers people do nothing and take an "it won't happen to me" approach.

The second barrier to change is that the threat is invisible, as is often the outcome. I mentioned earlier the visceral nature of terrorism, and the fact that it's highly visual. Like so many things, we understand what we can see, touch and feel – it's how we make sense of the world. Every day we read about another data breach. The Yahoo data breach, we have learnt, affected 3 billion...yes, 3 billion people, that's about 40% of the world's population. And recently we have seen Deloitte, Target and now Equifax also suffering breaches and data losses. What is also interesting is customer behaviour. Customers, despite knowing that their data has been stolen, remain with the company that was supposed to keep it secure. There is a remarkable lack of outrage from the very people who should rightly be outraged.

It may be because people no longer feel their data is precious or that if they change their password it will be ok. Perhaps it's because it's not visible, unlike a theft of personal physical property.

The policing of cybercrime in the widest sense is also a virtual game of whacka-mole with very small resources compared with the scale of the threat. We are still fighting cyber criminality on a geographic basis, with geographic laws, something the cyber criminals are unhindered by. There are some notable successes, though, including the recent NCA arrest and extradition from Germany of a Briton accused of using an infected network of computers, called the "Mirai#14 botnet" to attack and blackmail Lloyds and Barclays. But everyone knows we can't arrest our way out of cyber criminality.

Brad Smith is Microsoft's president and chief legal officer. He has spoken before about the need for a Digital Geneva Convention to address state sponsored cyber attacks, a digital non-proliferation treaty for cybercrime, if you will. Again, the non-visible attack vector needs more than separate countries responding geographically.

The penalties for being breached are also going to change the game when the General Data Protection Regulation (GDPR) comes into force in March 2018, with the highest fines at Euro 20 million or 4% of annual turnover, not profit. In the UK, the Information Commissioner's Office (ICO) can fine up to £500k. Talk Talk, for its data breach, was fined £400k, a small price, many would argue, for the way it was handled. If the GDPR had been in place then it could have been £59m. Sanctions on companies will force cultural change.

Heavily regulated sectors such as finance have long been aware of the penalties for transgression, and have invested heavily to ensure they are working within the conditions required by their regulators. GDPR will change the regulatory framework further, and, for those sectors not used to a strong regulatory oversight, particularly ISPs, telcos and retail, it is time for them ensure that all is done to protect themselves from cyber attack and data breaches.

And what can be done? If you look at some of the recent cyber attacks, patching was a common theme. And still many companies don't patch, often for months after the patch was issued. And what is a patch? Quite simply it's to fix a known vulnerability in your system. But because it can't be seen it's often not prioritised. If someone said your company's hot water system valve was about to blow, which could burn your employees, but here is a fix, you would get it done quickly, but for patching there is sometimes no organisational urgency. Many SMEs outsource their IT and network security – is patching a key contract requirement? And what's the "zero to patch" timeframe? It's your data, remember.

Patching isn't the only big ticket item, but if you can fix a vulnerability that's known, then a whole host of other issues may never come your way, you will have reduced your risk and demonstrated to the regulator, for instance, that you are taking things seriously. The former CEO of Equifax, Richard Smith, speaking to a US House Committee in October 2017 said, "Both the human deployment of the patch and the scanning deployment did not work." Human error? Seems a lot of responsibility on one person's shoulders, but in essence the lack of patching led to a breach and a whole lot more trouble leading to a data loss affecting 145 million people. Rep. Joe Barton (R-TX) said, "Under current law, you're required to alert those whose account has been hacked, but there's basically no penalty, we're going to have this hearing every year from now on if we don't do something to change this system."

Then there is the issue of the threats from within, the insider. Companies hire people and provide no familiarisation with what they can and can't do on company computers and equipment. Every new employee should have a half day where they are given a briefing on the dos and don'ts and the whys. And social engineering linked to all those social media accounts will make you a prime target for a phishing attack; just one click on a link and your company network is infected, the company offline, profits are falling, because the new employee just didn't know. It's not their fault, but I am certain they got an input on fire safety on the first day. Once again, the physical / visible risk is taking priority. You can't do everything; just as counter terrorism focuses on the priority threats it is the same here. Do you consider what your most important asset that needs protecting first is? Is it customer data, your client communication systems, power for your business's process or highly valuable intellectual property? Once you know what it is then you can think about protecting it and focus on what capital outlay you can afford to do it.

What simple steps can you take? The insider threat again: do you allow employees to plug in removable media or phones to charge in the USB slot? Or do you, like in an organisation I once worked for, superglue the slots up? Simple and crude but it works. Understanding what the risks are is crucial, and that doesn't always require techie speak. Your employees may not like it, but your company will be safer and so will their jobs in the long-term.

And now the criminals are getting insiders to launch phishing attacks on fellow employees from within. Fair usage policy at work allows employees to go from shopping on the Internet to work email in three clicks. We all want our employees to feel at home while at work, which is great but there are risks which need to be thought about.

The advice available to people on cyber security is, in my opinion, still too noisy, akin to the first diamond prospectors just sifting and hoping, with no real science. The NCSC is, however, starting to provide pragmatic advice to companies, especially SMEs, where cybercrime volume is a risk. The CyberSecurity Information Sharing Partnership (CISP), part of CERT-UK, is a joint industry-government initiative to share cyber threats and vulnerability information in order to increase overall situational awareness of the cyber threat and therefore reduce the impact on UK businesses. This too is a good place for an SME to start and growing memberships give SMEs greater resilience by working together to prevent cyber attacks.

National standards on cybersecurity products are also something that could help people as they walk the cyber highway. Just as you can't buy a plug without a kite mark, a car without an NCAP rating nor should you be able to buy some cyber protection products which haven't at least been assessed independently. Appetite, at least centrally from the state, is not there yet. The closest is Cyber Essentials but only go to the official site as there are lots of "experts" selling those silver bullets. **https://www.cyberaware.gov.uk/cyberessentials**

To sum it up, the wait and see approach has had its day and it is a confusing place, but to get visual understanding I have always broken it down in my head into a physical simile. Recent events show that it's not a case of if but when and when it comes have you done all that you can that is reasonable? Have you patched? Considered and responded to the insider threat? Asked the techies to explain in simple language? Taken the advice from NCSC? Joined a CISP? If you have you are already on the cyber protection highway; if you haven't, you are on a muddy path littered with hidden obstacles just waiting for you to step on them…

1.4 CYBERSECURITY: MOVING FROM AWARENESS TO UNDERSTANDING

Mark Barmby, PA Consulting Group

Effective cybersecurity is not a new business issue. It has been high on the board agenda of many large companies for some time. There have been enough high profile incidents in recent years to mean that senior leaders are well aware of the risks, and the costs, of any failure to manage them effectively. Yet, too often, that awareness is not translated into a real understanding of the threat they face.

Part of the problem is that cybersecurity is complex; the threats and technology are constantly evolving and business models are always being transformed to meet shifting customer expectations. However, instead of trying to understand that complexity, many organisations look for oversimplified solutions. There is a tendency to take a one dimensional approach to cybersecurity and assume that the problem is a technical one and so can be solved by technical applications. This is simply not the case. To build truly effective cyber defences requires a whole range of human and organisational responses, alongside the technical ones.

Companies should not assume that because they are spending a lot on cyber security products they are well protected. Instead, they should develop more holistic approaches based on a detailed understanding of how their business generates value and how to protect the elements that are critical to success.

UNDERSTAND THE DEPENDENCIES

Organisations should start by identifying the critical parts of their operations that depend on IT. From corner shops with digital cash registers, to airlines with online check-in and baggage management systems, it is hard to think of any modern organisation that is not highly dependent on IT systems. Yet many of them continue to lack understanding of the risks this brings, or fail to communicate those risks across the organisation.

The starting point of any cybersecurity plan has to be effective identification of risk, and there are plenty of tools available to support this work. Value chain mapping, which helps commercial organisations identify all the activities necessary to generate revenue, and therefore what needs to be protected. Fault tree analysis is another helpful tool that works backwards from a worst case scenario to understand how it could have happened. While event tree analysis works the other way round by looking at minor events and their potential consequences.

These relatively simple processes can be used to help identify which functions are critical to what the organisation does and the effect of any failure on that activity. It is important to recognise that each will have a different kind of value to protect. For a supermarket, a failure that results in an inability to process payments at the cash registers would remove their ability to generate revenue and destroy value if it took time to restore the service. In contrast, in an organisation that held sensitive personal data, a lack of availability of the service for a short time would be less damaging than losing the data and compromising customers' privacy.

Timing also matters. Losing access to HR systems would normally just be inconvenient. However, losing access to payroll data when staff were about to be paid might cause significant problems, reducing employees' confidence in their employer and causing financial hardship.

Any value chain analysis should also develop an understanding of the interdependencies between the different parts of the organisation. The collapse of British Airway's IT systems in May 2017 is a powerful example of the damage that can be caused by not identifying and reducing interdependencies. An accidental unplugging of the power supply in the data centre brought down the airline's entire online check-in, baggage handling and customer contact systems. This resulted in 700 flights being cancelled and cost BA £80 million, along with significant reputational damage reaching far beyond the 75,000 passengers affected directly. Had they understood the interdependency of these systems, followed industry best practice, and taken action to mitigate the risks, the impact of the problem would have been much less severe.

UNDERSTAND WHAT IS IMPORTANT

It is clear that many organisations have not carried out a fundamental review of what is really important to their operations. We can see the effect of this in the way the UK's National Health Service (NHS) handled the WannaCry virus in May 2017. Initially, the response was focused on assuring patients that no sensitive data had been lost. Yet, it soon became clear that the true impact of the attack was being felt by patients who had treatment cancelled. As IT systems were shut down to prevent the virus spreading, departments stopped working and 19,000 appointments were cancelled because hospitals were unable to, or unprepared to, continue without the IT systems.

The failure to treat patients was more damaging than the potential loss of data but all the effort was going into protecting the data. As the UK's National Audit Office report into the incident noted:

"The WannaCry cyber attack had potentially serious implications for the NHS and its ability to provide care to patients. It was a relatively unsophisticated attack and could have been prevented by the NHS following basic IT security best practice."

Focusing on the wrong things happens regularly in the aftermath of cyber incidents as organisations lose sight of what they exist to do and where their value lies. This also makes it harder to recover from an attack. If a restaurant cash register system crashes at lunchtime, the best option for avoiding financial loss would be to deal with the transactions manually using a printed price list. Yet an organisation without a proper plan and understanding of what matters will tend to divert all the attention to restoring the IT and ignore its customers.

This underlines that understanding and removing any critical dependencies can be a highly effective and inexpensive way to manage a cyber event. While this may change, most organisational functions today existed before computerisation, so having a clear and tested back-up process should be the easiest way to mitigate cyber incidents.

KEEP FOCUSED

The reality is that even organisations with a clear understanding of their vulnerabilities need to ensure they remain focused on evolving threats and growing value. Maintaining that focus is difficult when there are many more immediate requirements to update and develop IT systems and processes.

This is a particular risk now due to the impact of the European Union's General Data Protection Regulation (GDPR). This will require fundamental changes in how organisations manage and retain data, and the costs of noncompliance are high. Yet it is important that this work does not distract from the wider requirement to protect the business from cyber attack.

There is a real risk that companies could end up with excellent GDPR compliance but will have neglected their cyber defences and ultimately exposed their customers to greater risk. The GDPR should not become a tick box exercise but should be implemented in a manner that improves the overall way companies manage personal data and the experience of their customers.

For example, financial services providers could offer specific privacy settings for customers to opt into when they access services. Putting power in the hands of the customer in this way not only ensures compliance but also creates trust that the company is taking data privacy seriously.

CYBERSECURITY IS NOT JUST AN IT PROBLEM

None of this will be possible unless there is a wider acceptance that cybersecurity is an organisation-wide problem, not just an IT problem. In too many organisations, the IT department still does not know how to talk to the business, and the business does not listen to what the IT department is telling them.

The TalkTalk cyber attack in 2015 is a powerful illustration of how an IT problem rapidly became a business problem. The company reportedly ended up taking a £60m financial hit, including a £400,000 fine (a figure that would have been much higher if the GDPR had been in place). They also saw a 25 per cent drop in shareholder value and a significant loss of customers. Dido Harding, the CEO at the time, tried to get on the front foot by appearing on television to reassure customers, but it soon became clear that she did not understand the technical side of the problem. In particular, she was unable to provide an accurate answer to the critical question of whether customer data had been encrypted, arguably exacerbating an already challenging business problem.

This could be avoided by companies providing opportunities for IT teams to explain the technical aspects of a cyber incident to their business leaders, and coaching them in how to frame the problem in a language that resonates with the senior team. Equally, leaders need to make sure they truly understand the technical aspects of what they are being told and have a plan for communicating this information.

LOOK BEYOND TECHNOLOGY

Only by being well informed will leaders be able to make effective decisions about their approach. No-one can afford to defend everything, the same way, all the time, so they have to ensure that the right weaknesses are prioritised and mitigated. This means resisting the temptation simply to buy more technical solutions. All too often businesses end up with technical capability but do not know how, where or why to employ it.

Technical measures can only ever be one part of a cybersecurity plan. Employees are a critical part of any organisation's defences. Yet, while most of them are aware of the risks, very few truly have the level of understanding they need to avoid falling victim to phishing and social engineering based attacks which remain the major vulnerability for organisations.

To address this there needs to be a real improvement in developing employee understanding. Sitting them in a classroom for an hour, and taking them through the cyber risks will not give them the understanding of the risks they face, and the mistakes they can make. Companies should adopt far more imaginative approaches that truly empower employees by giving them real up to date knowledge and experience of how to identify and handle threats.

FACE THE REALITY

A central point in understanding cybersecurity is accepting the inevitability of an attack. Successful cyber defence requires honesty about the risks and potential impacts of cyber incidents and a willingness to assume the worst can happen.

The problem is that Chief Information Officers are often reluctant to conduct cyber-resilience tests. They can be afraid of what they might discover, or over optimistic about how easily their business can recover. But it is only by testing that organisations can truly understand how well prepared they are.

There also needs to be a clear recognition that attackers can afford to be patient, they can afford to fail multiple times, they can probe and test from many directions, and they can wait until they get a lucky break. They will also have a very good sense of what is valuable to a business because they want to steal or destroy it.

Well conducted testing will reveal flaws not just in IT processes but across the business, in areas such as communications, staff management and overall business plans. Only by exposing these problems can the organisation take steps to address them.

IMPLEMENT THE PLAN

When an attack happens, it is vital to implement a tested plan while remembering the military saying that *'no plan survives first contact with the enemy'*[1]. That means having clear ways to change the plan while ensuring leaders are adequately and fully informed and understand the impact of any action.

For larger organisations, SOCs can be an effective way to ensure recovery plans are implemented. If they work well, they will be able to deploy the right threat intelligence, gather the right data, and apply the right analytics to respond quickly and appropriately. For them to do this, they will need to have a clear understanding of the organisational context and the value chain mapping that has been done. If the security analysts do not understand the organisation they are trying to protect, they risk responding to the wrong threats in the wrong way.

PREPARE FOR THE FUTURE

Even if organisations get all this right today, they need to understand that these solutions will not necessarily be effective next month or next year. Cybersecurity has always been an evolving problem, but that evolution is accelerating. The ever increasing amount of data that needs to be monitored and protected is soon going to be beyond most current SOCs. A recent survey found that 93% of SOCs are unable to

---

1. Paraphrased from Prussian military strategist Field Marshal Helmuth Karl Bernhard Graf von Moltke.

triage all potential threats because the volume of incoming alerts is overwhelming[2].

However, this is one area where technology can offer solutions. Some organisations are beginning to use artificial intelligence and machine learning to create systems that can carry out more sophisticated monitoring of behaviour. These are better able to spot anomalies and changes in behaviour, such as an employee logging in from a different machine or at a different time or location from usual. Of course, this kind of monitoring raises both broad ethical issues and specific HR challenges. Investigating an employee for an innocent change in working pattern might not be the best response. It might be an opportunity to understand why that employee put security at risk and how the systems or processes might have made that happen.

Another future cybersecurity challenge is the arrival into the workforce of a new generation that is much more used to sharing information and using their own devices in the workplace. Companies will need to find ways of accommodating those different attitudes and ways of working without compromising security.

CONCLUSION

The fact that cyber attacks keep happening and keep destroying value means it is easy to be pessimistic about our ability to tackle them. It is true that too many organisations still do not understand the full complexity of their value chain or how they generate revenue and do not have a plan to defend it. Some still do not understand that they need to focus on defending the value chain rather than simply defending their networks and systems. That task is not going to get any easier as attackers will constantly find new ways to achieve their aims.

The National Cyber Security Centre now provides good and easy to implement advice for all sizes of business. They support a clear process where businesses truly understand the interdependencies and what is important, and use this information to develop and implement realistic and effective plans. Organisations will also need to continue to seek expert advice on the best technology and business design to help them to deal with these evolving threats.

If leaders can take these steps to move their awareness of the problem to a real understanding of the risks, they will stand a chance of getting ahead of the attackers.

---

2. https://www.recordedfuture.com/security-operations-center-strategy/

1.5 HOW CYBER CRIMINALS MAKE MONEY

Nick Ioannou, Boolean Logical Ltd

While there is no limit to a cyber criminal's creativity, ranging from sophisticated scams to an automated bot army to do their bidding, there are generally only four main ways they make money. So regardless of the technological methods or psychological tricks employed, it will generally be either via extortion, fraud, theft, or unauthorised use of your assets and these can also be mixed or combined together for maximum effect. Each way offers a differing expectation of the amount of time before the criminal is paid, or facilitates the others. Extortion generally is the quickest as the criminals get paid directly, together with time restrictions for the victim. Fraud is next, while theft is often the slowest, as the criminals often need to sell the data they have stolen, use mules to launder the money or reuse the data for extortion or fraud. Unauthorised use of your assets generally facilitates extortion, theft and fraud, often directed at external third parties as well as your own systems.

So by understanding how cyber criminals make money and the psychological tricks they employ, we can identify the gaps and risks in our systems, raise awareness and put in place more effective security controls. Let's look each of the four ways in more detail.

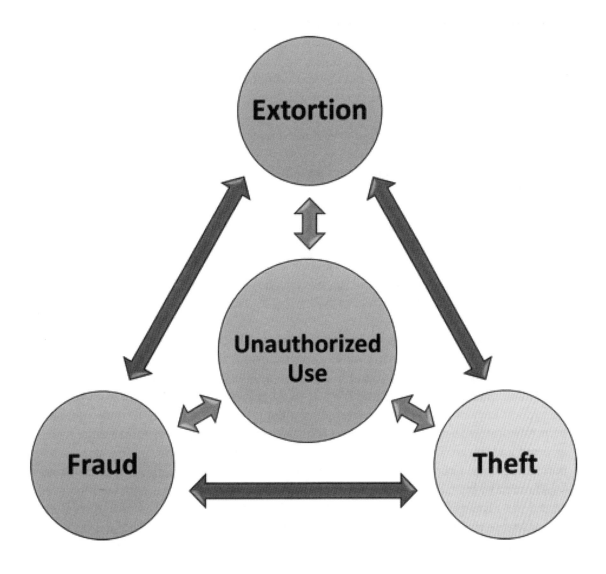

EXTORTION - PAYMENTS YOU ARE FORCED INTO MAKING

Extortion is basically summed up by one of two questions put to the victim – either 'pay up or there will be consequences' or 'pay up to make it stop.' It offers criminals an immediate income as the victims are asked to pay via crypto-currencies within a defined timeframe after which the ransom is increased, the severity of the consequences increased or the ability to roll back the consequences is no longer an option. The most common types of cyber extortion are:

- Ransomware has encrypted your data and you will need to pay to get the encryption keys to recover it;

- Ransomware has locked you out of your computer and you will need to pay via another machine to get access;

- Ransom demand to not share data obtained by fraud or theft;

- Ransom demand to not share data you thought was private (e.g. compromising photos or videos);

- Ransom demand to stop a denial of service attack (DDoS attack) on your infrastructure;

- Ransom demand based on scare tactics and lies to trick the victim, or potential for consequences, whether real or fake.

Incentives to pay may include the threat of permanently deleting your data or rendering your computer unusable. Paying an extortion ransom, though, has no guarantee that the criminal will carry out their end of the deal, although the odds are they will if it is a fully automated ransomware infection. If word gets out that they do not give you the encryption keys or access to your computer, then it affects their long term income. To help, ransomware has evolved where some include a limited file decryption feature to act as proof and, bizarrely, help desks you can contact to guide you through the process of purchasing crypto-currencies and the steps to remove the 'consequences' of the ransom.

There have been cases, though, with denial of service ransoms against companies, where the victims have paid up yet the attack eases up slightly but still continues. According to the cyber criminals that were paid, they held up their end of the bargain, but unbeknownst to the victim a second cyber criminal was still attacking them. Whether true or not, it does make good business sense from a criminal's point of view to attack a company that is already being attacked. It will be harder for the victim to mitigate and they will be more likely to pay.

Also, ransom demands can be made purely on threats alone, without the cyber criminals actually needing to do anything. So long as the victim believes the criminal has infected their systems, or has the resources to attack them and cause disruption, the extortion attempt can work. The criminal then has the potential to use the premise of the first fake consequence to get the victim to infect themselves for real under the guise of a fix, after which the whole cycle starts again.

Lastly, ransom demands can be particularly nasty, like the Petya and NotPetya ransomware viruses, which relied on an exploited system flaw to initially infect machines, then quickly spread across the network to machines that were patched against the initial flaw. A brutal payment request is displayed on an already unusable machine which no longer starts correctly and in many cases was worthless as there was no way to reverse the damage, even if you paid the ransom. But it did not stop there, as encryption of your documents and files allowed a second round of extortion once you got your machine working again.

FRAUD – PAYMENTS YOU ARE TRICKED INTO MAKING

Discovering you have been conned, defrauded or tricked, however you phrase it, it is not a pleasant experience. Cyber fraud is much harder to stop, though, because digital assets can be easily copied from websites of companies and organisations and then repurposed by the criminals. There is no ID requirement to setup an email address or get a pay-as-you-go mobile phone, and with these you can create accounts on social media networks and deploy cloud services. This allows the criminals to create a convincing backdrop to facilitate their fraud attempts, that with a bit of effort can be practically indistinguishable from the genuine one. Luckily many criminals do not put much effort in, so by being vigilant and checking that the domain name and any hyperlinks are genuine and looking for small mistakes, you can spot most fraudulent emails and websites.

The most common types of cyber fraud are:

- Advanced fee fraud (admin fee to claim a competition prize, solicitor fee for inheritance)

- Fake service payment (fake road tax website or subscription renewal)

- IT support telephone scams

- Fake invoice payment

- Fake software purchase or upgrade

- Fake online casino

- Fake financial investment product

- Fake excess fee owed (parcel delivery).

Many fraud victims never find out they have been a victim, while others realise weeks later. Either way, it's better to know than not know, otherwise you can fall for the same scam again. As soon as you realise you have been defrauded, work out what information you have given to the criminals and take steps to reduce the value of that information where possible, for instance cancel any credit cards used to pay them and contact your bank or payment provider to make sure there are no repeat payments scheduled.

Never pay anything via a link in an email where possible and instead manually go to the vendor's website and login with your account credentials. The same applies for anyone that calls you and then asks for payment before they proceed to 'help you'; instead, ask them for their name and department (but not their telephone number) then look up their contact information on the company website. If you can, use a different phone line, otherwise call your own mobile or someone you know to confirm the line has been cleared.

THEFT

The incredible speed of the internet that is now available to most people allows criminals to steal data from their victims without them realising, as what would have previously taken hours can now take seconds. Whether the victim inadvertently enters their credentials or financial information into a fake website, a key logger captures their key strokes or a Trojan uploads their files, the result is the same.

The most common types of cyber theft are:

* ID theft

* Credential theft (usernames and passwords)

* Financial theft

* Data theft

The stolen information is either sold on to other criminals or used to facilitate extortion, fraud or unauthorised use of assets. Months can go by without you realising anything is amiss if the criminals choose to be stealthy and often it is a third party that informs you that you have been compromised.

As with fraud, as soon as you realise you have been a victim of data theft, it is important to work out what information the criminals may have and take steps to reduce the value of that information where possible, for instance, changing passwords and reviewing account details for password recovery emails in case they have been changed. Also, establishing what has been stolen is no easy task when it comes to data theft and will depend on how well your security systems log outbound activities. The criminals do not have to target the primary live systems to commit data theft, but instead go after the backups and secondary systems, including cloud backups. So through credential theft, a criminal can move to data theft via a cloud backup and there may be nothing to investigate on the primary systems. Robust logging of all your systems can help alert you to unusual internet traffic, but a determined and patient criminal who is already in your systems is extremely hard to stop.

UNAUTHORISED USE

Criminals do not want to pay for global IT infrastructure or data bandwidth so they use yours instead. When they compromise a computer or device they have one of two choices: option one – exploit the machine to extort, trick or steal from the owner, or option two – exploit the machine to commit extortion, fraud or theft on others. Individually your computer resources are quite limited, but when hundreds of thousands are linked together to form a Botnet, the available computing resources become vast. On the infected computers the users may be quite unaware of any symptoms other than the computer behaving slightly slower than usual. Assuming that is, that the inflected computer is one that has a screen and interface, as criminals also look at ways of infecting internet enabled devices like security cameras, smart devices and even home internet routers to do their bidding.

The most common types of unauthorised use are:

- Botnet for hire

- Ad fraud (click-jacking)

- Spam relay

- Denial of services attacks

- Crypto-currency mining

- Password brute forcer

- Virus propagation

- Web server

- Command and control server (C&C)

- Storage server

- Remote Access Trojan

What is important to understand is that the criminals can decide to stop using the resources of your machine and change tack at any time, as they effectively have full control of your machine. So what might start out as unauthorised use could quickly change to theft, fraud or extortion.

Also, the criminals are not restricting themselves to what most people traditionally think of as computers. They are quite happy to compromise practically anything with a computer inside which is hooked up to the internet. We know these as SMART devices or the Internet of Things (IoT), and despite appearing to be low powered, they are perfect for the criminals and unfortunately for us, there are billions of these things out there, with little or next to no security.

Now to make matters worse, extortion, fraud and theft can also be a springboard to each other, as criminals are resourceful like that.

THEFT LEADING TO EXTORTION

The new General Data Protection Regulation (GDPR) laws coming into effect in May 2018 bizarrely give criminals an extortion opportunity for personal data they have illegally obtained. The threat of the potentially huge fines and resulting negative press can be used to extort money from companies in order to keep the breach of their systems quiet. So long as the ransom demand is significantly less than what a potential fine could be, companies may decide to go with the lesser pain and pay the ransom, especially if the criminals provide evidence that the company were incompetent and could have easily protected themselves better, which would raise the chance of a fine. Once you pay, though, there is no guarantee they will not ask for money again or renege on their side of the deal and go public with both the breach and the fact you paid to cover it up. There is still the good old fashion extortion based on not disclosing something in the stolen data, which could be anything from personally compromising emails from board members, dubious activities, evidence of incompetence, or plain old trade secrets.

FRAUD LEADING TO EXTORTION

After the criminals have tricked a victim into paying for a fake service or product, the victim will be expecting to receive an email receipt or invoice, and some criminals will use this to deliver a ransomware or Trojan virus to them. There is also extortion via the threat of disclosing that the victim was negligent to their senior management and directly responsible for enabling the fraud.

EXTORTION LEADING TO THEFT

One of the easiest ways to enter a secure area is get someone on the inside with the necessary privileges to let you in, or to give you their keys and access codes. The same applies to cybersecurity, though in this case it could be asking an employee that the criminals have some hold over to install a remote access Trojan or create a new account with admin credentials for the criminals. A ransomware virus could also include a credential theft module, like the NotPetya virus, which would pass administrator credentials and login info to the criminals. Data theft is also an option, so as well as encrypting your data, some ransomware will also copy your data to a cloud based repository.

FRAUD LEADING TO THEFT

Criminals like to pay for goods with your money, not theirs, so after handing over all your credit card and delivery address information on a fake website, they can then go online shopping. All the criminals have to do is be there as the courier arrives and requesting that the courier calls a pay-as-you-go mobile before they arrive makes this relatively easy. I've know of a case where two new Apple iMac computers arrived in a business loading bay and disappeared before the real person, who didn't know they had paid for them, found out.

EXTORTION LEADING TO FRAUD

It is quite easy for criminals to reuse payment information given to them as part of an extortion attempt, or to sell it on to other criminals. The criminals can also pose as a helpful company monitoring this particular extortion and sell you a new service to mitigate future attempts of their own extortion.

THEFT LEADING TO FRAUD

Cyber criminals need online identities to function, namely email addresses, credit cards and physical addresses, for which they are quite happy to use someone else's. This is where an online database breach can give the criminals hundreds of thousands (if not millions) of online identities to work with. It can also lead to criminals cold calling or emailing posing as debt collectors and taking payments for services that are not actually in arrears.

IN SUMMARY

So now we know what we are trying to protect against, we can raise our colleagues' awareness and start to close the advantage gap the criminals have. Cybersecurity is all about stopping extortion, fraud, theft and unauthorised use, which is a lot easier to understand and get budget approval. If you focus on stopping unauthorised use, it helps everyone else too!

1.6 IF SMES ARE THE LIFE BLOOD OF THE BRITISH ECONOMY, WE'VE CUT AN ARTERY

Brian Lord, PGI Group

THE BRITISH CYBER SECURITY SYSTEM SIMPLY DOESN'T HELP SMES

The most frustrating, patronising, and ill-informed regular comment that emerges whenever a group of cyber security consultants and practitioners are put together is: "… companies have to understand that cyber security is a business enabler…".

Sigh. To every business, of any size, cyber security is an overhead; just like other security risks, it has always been an overhead, and it will always be an overhead. And to every business person there is a single rule regarding overheads. Keep them as low as you possibly can. Start at £0.00 and build upwards – only accepting the absolute essential after heavy scrutiny.

And before those cyber security experts throw their hands up in horror and bemoan how that is because "they don't really understand the risk or threat…", I can safely say that most DO understand the threat – at a headline level at least. Cyber security specialists care passionately about their area of expertise: it is the most important risk in their lives. Business owners simply care about it alongside all the other risks inherent in running a business, many of which have a greater proximity and risk of damage. It doesn't make it unimportant, it simply takes its place alongside other risks.

This overhead rule applies to all businesses, but to Small and Medium Enterprises (SMEs), it is often the difference between business success and failure. The reason SMEs don't buy cyber security services is not because they aren't aware of the threat or risk, it is because there is no clarity whatsoever over what they actually need to protect them from the specific risk they face. Moreover, the price tag that comes with whatever services they actually do try to pursue is so eye-wateringly expensive it puts them beyond reach.

Many SMEs often carry on trading and operating unprotected because so few organisations are prepared to help deliver them what they need, in the form they need, at a price they need. This of course significantly undermines the admirable UK Government's aspiration to make the UK 'the safest place in the world to do business'. But perhaps more significantly, it continues to facilitate an opportunistic and mass criminal free-for-all which dilutes and distracts the ability and capacity of limited national law enforcement and intelligence resources to counter what is an evolving and mutating threat. We are still some way away from a UK where "petty" cyber theft has become just too difficult to carry out at scale, and thus allows national resources to be focussed on the deeper more malevolent criminals and threat actors. And we are probably about three years behind where we should be at this point.

So, where and how does this square become circled? Let's look at the four corners of those who can help. Firstly, the Government (in the form of the National Cyber Security Centre [NCSC] and other government bodies), who still struggle to understand the world of the SME. Secondly, the cyber security industry, who still prefer to keep their nose in the trough, only serving those who can pay the preposterous prices they charge and doing everything possible to preserve the status quo. Thirdly, the large corporate industry, who can reduce their own risk from a supply chain of SMEs and an SME client base, through facilitating and supporting measures. Finally, there are the SMEs themselves whose cyber security stasis simply cannot continue.

GOVERNMENT

The NCSC, now a year old, has a department dedicated to the SME market. Just last month, they launched the hugely digestible *Small Business Guide to Cyber Security*, aimed at giving straightforward advice to SMEs as to how they should address the threat in a way that made sense and was affordable to them. It is clear, it is concise, but still focusses on technical controls and it is very unlikely that most SMEs will be able to implement the measures suggested without some alternative help and advice (back to the affordability again). And if we consider beyond the technical controls to the primary vulnerability of the human, it was only in May this year that Joe Siegrist, the VP of Last Pass, called upon the NCSC to produce some education for small businesses, and there still remains a large gap in education (rather than availability of information) that needs to be promulgated and made available to SMEs. The point being is it wouldn't take too much of the £1.9 billion allocated to the National Cyber Security Programme (certainly no more than 1%) to make cyber security education available to the 99.3% (2016 figures) of all UK businesses, who produce 47% of the UK private sector turnover. (Federation of Small Businesses, 2017).

But these measures are destined to stay in the realm of facilitation, rather than intervention. So where else can the UK Government adopt a policy approach that reflects the realities of the SME world, where the rules and considerations are different to public sector organisations and large industry?

Government standards, certification and accreditations continue to emerge out of the NCSC (previously CESG) with the laudable intent of providing something against which the private sector can measure what is good when they buy or assume protective measures and services. However, there appears to be an inability to differentiate what really is the skill level and certification standard necessary to measure service levels to a large complex organisation and that are required by the majority of SMEs. 'Gold Standard' or not, obtaining these certifications and accreditations continues to be hugely bureaucratic and very expensive for service deliverers to obtain and sustain. As we will see (below), these organisations need no excuse to justify extraordinarily high prices.

We recognise that it requires high-end and complex skills and knowledge to protect parts of the Critical National Infrastructure, and so means of certifying these to a reassuringly high level are right. But what is lacking is a set of routine, affordable service benchmarks which help an SME determine the difference between 'cowboy' and 'competent' and measure what:

(a) is good enough to protect them;

(b) assures their insurer that responsible judgements have been made (because, yes, insurance is the primary mitigation measure);

and

(c) demonstrates to the ICO, should the worst case scenario happen, that they took reasonable and informed measures to meet their legal and regulatory responsibilities.

If the SME department of the NCSC achieves anything in the coming year, it would be to drive a coach and horses through the self-licking certification and accreditation lollipop and set some affordable standards for services and training to SMEs. This would take a massive step forward in defining and creating an affordable envelope for SME cyber security standards.

The NCSC is a force for good, but needs help in understanding exactly what drives an SME's decision making.

THE CYBER SECURITY INDUSTRY

Ever since 1999 and the Y2K cash cow, the IT security/information security/cyber security industry has rubbed its hands, over-complicated and over-teched the risk and threat, bought the national supply of mirrors and smoke and proceeded to try to create a fear culture that has simply served to produce a stasis and drag on proportionate adoption and normalisation of measures. And along the way led CESG by the nose in the co-creation of a cyber world of over-complicated standards, skills, service levels and faux-qualification hierarchies.

The argument put forward is that there are too few qualified people to meet the national demand for skills and certification. Basic economics lays out the straightforward concept of supply and demand on cost and sale. The skills and certification levels are co-created by the Government, who have an altruistic reason to make the nation safe, and an IT/cyber security industry who want to make a lot of money. When it comes to protecting critical infrastructure and organisations against whom there is a multi-layered threat, it is quite right that standards are very high and, as in all professions, the highest skills demand the highest prices.

But SMEs look on and wonder why they seem to have to pay a doctor or a surgeon to deal with a cut finger, or help avoid catching flu. The information (and the pricing point) available seems not to differentiate much between the equivalent of a First Aider, a St John's Ambulance Officer, a Nurse, a GP, a Senior House Officer, a Registrar, a Surgeon and a Consultant. And there is no benefit to industry in explaining there could be a difference. Not being able to afford it, the SMEs go away with no idea how to stop catching flu and their finger's still cut. And of course, many catch flu and their fingers go septic and have to return to a smug "I told you so" doctor and surgeon. Q.E.D.

But it seems there should be no real downside to creating a more dynamic and flexible approach to these issues in a way that helps an SME afford to counter what is a persistent 21st century threat. Well, inevitably there is a risk that the very large multi-national companies and CNI providers, who do pay top dollar, will then realise that not ALL their cyber security risks need to be dealt with at the same level and could readjust downwards accordingly.

One of the leading organisations trying to supply affordable services to SMEs, the London Digital Security Centre (LDSC), has a number of service delivery partners. However, with the honourable exception of Sophos and Symantec (since the AV vendors matured and grew out of scaremongering pricing several years ago), the number of major providers of cyber security products, consultancy and services are noticeable by their absence.

In October this year the LDSC took themselves to Birmingham to demonstrate the model and provide the same type of help they routinely offer to London SMEs. The issue remains not one of just providing information – but one of implementing practical solutions, including training that allows SMEs to protect themselves in an affordable, continuous and sustainable way.

Development of automated services, including on-line training, testing, protection, certification, maturity modelling and online Information Security Management Systems remains the end-state for the bulk of the SME market. And it is only when the industry service providers can branch out from rarefied gold-plated selling and apply a pragmatic solution to a basic model, with appropriate, proportionate and affordable kite-marking, delivered through an annuity revenue approach, will the SME market really be able to protect itself... And the ability to reach a market of that scale needs to be through an increased national number of public and private bodies, such as the LDSC, in which the large service providers will play properly, at the right price, with staff at the right level of skills to conduct the level of work required.

With the right model, within three years the not-for-profit nature of such bodies would have developed a cultural change within both the providers and the SME market to become a largely privately funded body, able to release the public funds back into public services. This is not altruism, it is a hard, commercial fact – there is an untapped market in annuitised, online solutions, like all services that help manage risk for SMEs. A solution of this type remains the only viable solution, but it is a solution that can be extremely profitable to those who deliver and affordable to those who buy. It just requires industry noses to be lifted out of a shallow trough, in which the food is rapidly going stale.

WIDER INDUSTRY

One of the most enlightening afternoons I have had recently, was when we invited a number of large industry partners to our offices and Cyber Academy. These partners were those who recruited their own cyber security professionals, either to work internally on their own corporate protection or those who could deliver services for others. The purpose was to launch our skills conversion programme through which they could recruit new members of staff who would become operationally viable (i.e. deliver independent cyber security capability) within 10 weeks. Not the "gold standard" (see below) but the basic, more procedural, systemic implementation that is an inherent part of any security process or compliance based service delivery.

As we wheeled out our own staff who had gone through our own similar internal programme, and were already delivering cyber security effect, the scales fell and the disbelief was suspended as it became hugely apparent to them that the cheque book recruitment they had hitherto been undertaking was not wholly necessary, and there were cheaper more effective routes through which the skills shortage could be addressed.

It doesn't just make obvious commercial sense for the companies concerned, but it also halts a strand of cheque book recruitment, which creates disproportionately high salaries which are passed on to the clients, place it out of reach of the SME market and limit the corporate willingness to build cheaper, more annuitised services, as described above.

And from another angle, as wider industry looks, as it should, at where and how different levels of service standard should be applied to different parts of the business (i.e. where do they need a brain surgeon and where do they need a nurse), it becomes apparent that some of the swifter, cheaper, even annuitised models may be applicable to them in some part. It therefore becomes in their interest to ensure the development (and price) of such capability moves on apace.

So large corporate industry needs to look at how and where CSR and marketing budgets are currently being deployed in the cyber spaces, because, adopted smartly it will provide a return not only in profile and reputation, but it will massively reduce their own recruitment and service delivery costs, and take a major step towards influencing the speed at which their SME supply chain adopts sensible security measures that protect their own corporate assets and liabilities.

SMES THEMSELVES

While it remains absolutely imperative that the levels of service and solutions available to SMEs are proportionate and in line with the culture and business processes in the SME world, it is also not feasible to perpetuate the existing inertia in the SME world around protecting online assets and capability. The threat is inherent in the adoption of modern technologies which allow businesses to thrive in the 21st century. Now is the time to engage, both collectively and individually. The NCSC SME department, perhaps more than any other area of the organisation, depends upon input and engagement from those they seek to serve. Without it, they will get it wrong – not out of incompetence, but because they don't have the knowledge they seek for initiatives to work in the SME environment.

Engage in the bodies being set up, often with the help of the local police force, such as the LDSC, and take advantage of the services and support offered.

Be demanding from the cyber security industry. Collectively, through trade bodies, local business communities and other vehicles, challenge the pricing offered and demand more automated innovative solutions. Half an expensive solution is no solution at all.

It is a world in which SMEs will have to play, and only SMEs can really make the case for rules that work, because the rules of the game now aren't sustainable.

CONCLUSION

The current world of cyber security is not geared for SMEs. As already mentioned, the UK Government is investing 1.9 billion GBP into cyber security. (Osbourne, 2015). SMEs represent 99.3% of the private sector and generate 45% of the nation's private sector turnover at 1.8 trillion pounds. (Federation of Small Businesses, 2017). A comparatively small proportion of investment can secure a comparatively high proportion of UK economic interest.

The Government's aspiration can be met; the cyber security industry can thrive, larger industry can be better protected for less, and the SMEs themselves can have the levels of protection needed in the 21st century. All it needs is for the UK Government to be slightly more SME sensitive, the cyber security industry to work for its returns, wider industry to challenge the status quo and SMEs to understand how to make it all work for them. Because it isn't at the moment.

REFERENCE LIST

Federation of Small Businesses. (2017) *UK Small Business Statistics*. Available at: http://www.fsb.org.uk/media-centre/small-business-statistics (Accessed: 28 November 2017).

Osbourne, G. (2015) *Chancellor's Speech to GCHQ on Cyber Security*. Available at: https://www.gov.uk/government/speeches/chancellors-speech-to-gchq-on-cyber-security (Accessed: 28 November 2017).

Part Two

Addressing the Management Issues

2.1 MANAGING CYBER RISK: THE ROLE OF THE BOARD

Richard Knowlton, Richard Knowlton Associates

YOUR BUSINESS CANNOT FUNCTION WITHOUT CYBER RISK

Whatever your sector, your business depends heavily on digital technology.

HR, payroll and tax processes all run on computer programmes, while artificial intelligence is already handling routine tasks and driving your marketing and client management through "big data" analysis. If you are in the manufacturing or energy sectors, your production teams will be using robotics, industrial control systems and the so-called Internet of Things to drive a significant increased return on your investments.

The benefits of all this digital technology are so overwhelming that your business cannot work without it.

Inevitably there is a downside. Those indispensable digital systems can provide openings for criminals, hostile nation states and hackers who want to steal your data, disrupt your operations or just be a nuisance.

So while you cannot function without the cyber world, you also have to work with the risks that it brings.

WHY WOULD WE BE A TARGET?

If your business is relatively small, or does not hold much personal customer data, why would cyber attackers want to attack it?

Unfortunately, experience shows that hackers target organisations of all sizes and sectors. In fact, most cyber-attacks hit smaller organizations precisely because they have fewer security resources. Or perhaps you are a small cog in the supply chain of a much bigger and juicier target company. If so, hackers will look at your digital systems as a way into their real target.

CYBER SECURITY IS CHALLENGING...

Several factors make cyber security particularly challenging:

- *Complexity.* Even in smaller businesses you may use a variety of devices and computer systems. If your business has grown quickly through acquisition, you will have significant legacy issues around the secure integration of different systems and software.

- *Speed.* The digital world is rolling out at breakneck speed. Most businesses struggle to be as fleet-footed in security as the hackers are at breaking it down.

- *Scale.* Your company's computer systems may operate through extensive national or international networks. This increases efficiency, but it also increases the points of potential access for hackers.

- *Business models.* There is an unfortunate symmetry here:

    * Management often does not see security as a business priority: it only adds delay, cost and complexity.

    * Hacking is a great business model. Hackers need only a small investment of time and money to get a substantial return on investment. And their chances of being caught are vanishingly small.

- *Business needs.* Technical innovation and modern business practices (like 24/7 external access to data or complex international supply chains) greatly improve profitability. But they can also negatively impact cyber risk.

- *Asymmetric threats.* If cyber-attackers target your company, they will almost certainly get inside[1]. And they do not need to be that sophisticated.

- *Impact.* A major cyber incident in the health and energy sectors, for example, may lead to death or injury, or to a critical impact on the environment. Even "routine" cyber-attacks may lead to losses of hundreds of millions of pounds.

---

1. Companies may sometimes face the kind of sophisticated attacks that defeat governments, even in highly advanced countries. How is a business supposed to do better?

BUT THE SITUATION IS NOT HOPELESS...

Most successful cyber-attacks rely on poor discipline and processes in the target organisation. In fact, your employees, sub-contractors and others with access to your IT systems may pose a much bigger potential risk than an IT failure.

You will have heard some of the basic "hygiene" rules: never click on a link in a message unless you are sure where it has come from; use long and complex passwords and do not leave them where others can find them, and so on[2]. But in a pressured business environment, these simple rules are often forgotten. Or they have not been taught in the first place.

The good news is that companies really can drive down the risks from this human risk factor. A company that insists that security is at least as important as health and safety will be in a much better position to defend itself against cyber-attack.

A CONSISTENT BOARD APPROACH TO OVERSEEING CYBER RISK

Every company is different, and your Board's approach will vary according to your business's unique characteristics. However, all Boards of Directors need to apply a consistent approach to their oversight of cyber risk.

The following principles provide a framework to guide your thinking and to help you ask the right questions of your management.

1. Cyber risk management is not just a technical issue.

Too many organisations still make the fundamental mistake of seeing cyber security as a purely technical, operational issue. They delegate responsibility to their IT security department, a little-known "back-office" function often several layers away from strategic business decisions, and one that struggles for resources and budget.

If your company regards cyber security as a purely IT responsibility, then other parts of the business will not regard it as their problem. This inhibits critical analysis of security issues across the organisation, and inevitably hampers the implementation of your security strategy.

This is not to denigrate the role of IT specialists, whose expertise is an essential component of managing cyber risk. But never forget that many successful cyber-attacks exploit human and process weaknesses in your company's defences. These are not issues which management should simply leave to an IT department.

---

2. The UK National Cyber-Security Centre (NCSC) has excellent guidance on cyber hygiene (see https://www. ncsc.gov.uk/guidance).

2. Cyber security is part of your enterprise risk management process.

A successful cyber-attack on your company's systems represents a very serious risk to your business. You could suffer severe reputational damage and financial losses, not least through litigation and regulatory penalties. And you may lose intellectual property that has cost years of investment to develop.

It follows that cyber security issues must be a central part of your overall enterprise risk management process. The Board has a fundamental responsibility to ensure that your company is managing the risk in accordance with its importance. If you do not do this, you are leaving your company and its assets dangerously exposed.

Seen in this way, cyber risk sits directly alongside other enterprise risks that your Board is already well-used to reviewing (competition, tax exposure, regulation and so on).

3. Make sure that you have access to cyber risk expertise,

A recent government survey shows that far too many Boards still lack a clear understanding of the potential impacts of a cyber-attack (43%) and do not view cyber risk as a top risk (46%). Meanwhile, 68% of Boards say that they have received no training to deal with a cyber incident.[3]

How best to fill this knowledge gap at the Board level? There are various options, though clearly not all of them may be appropriate for your company:

- *Bring a cyber risk management expert* to the Board as a non-executive director or adviser.

- *Schedule "deep dive" briefings* with third party experts, including reputable cybersecurity consultants and industry associations. You should certainly take advice from the National Cyber Security Centre (NCSC).[4]

- *Leverage the Board's existing independent advisers.* External auditors, for example, will have a multi-client and industry-wide perspective on cyber risk trends.

---

3. See HM Government's "FTSE 350 Cyber Governance Health Check 2017" at https://www.gov.uk/government/publications/cyber-governance-health-check-2017.

4. "The NCSC was set up to help protect our critical services from cyber-attacks, manage major incidents, and improve the underlying security of the UK Internet through technological improvement and advice to citizens and organisations. Our vision is to help make the UK the safest place to live and do business online". See https://www.ncsc.gov.uk/information/about-ncsc.

- *Enrol Board members in director education programmes* covering cyber risk management issues.

4. Get cyber risk on to your agenda.

The government survey also found that 69% of UK Boards do not receive comprehensive and informative information on cyber risk from their management. Without that briefing, Boards cannot effectively oversee their management's cyber security strategies and priorities.

Your Board agenda should contain regular quality time for discussion of cyber issues. In this way, you will develop your knowledge of cyber risks in your organisation and of what is being done to mitigate their effects.

5. Understand the risks in your organisation.

You need detailed discussions with your management on the varying levels of cyber risk in your business. You can then agree an appropriate cyber risk posture and tolerance.

Where to start?

As a director, you should have a clear idea of your organisation's most valuable assets – the "crown-jewels" it most needs to protect. Where are these assets, and who has access to them? Is there adequate protection against a malicious attack on them? Can they ever be fully secure?

Having discussed these critical assets, ensure that your management has developed a security strategy that builds protection from the "crown jewels" outward. Has management considered how they will mitigate the effects of the highest probability attacks? What about the effects of those low-probability, high-impact attacks that could have catastrophic consequences?

In your early discussions, too, you need to be asking some direct questions of management, including the following:[5]

- How often have we been attacked so far? How did we find out? What were the impacts?

- Are we confident that when there is a significant cyber-attack, the Board will receive adequate information about it, including the nature of the breach, the

---

5. See the US National Association of Corporate Directors (NACD) publication "Cyber-risk Oversight" (Director's Handbook Series) – available at https://www.nacdonline.org/Store/ProductDetail.cfm?ItemNumber=10687. I contributed to the first edition of this publication (2014) as Group Corporate Security Director of Vodafone and Board member of the Internet Security Alliance (ISA).

data impacted, how management has responded, and the potential impacts on the company?

- What are our industry's best practices for cyber security? How do we compare?

- What are the biggest weaknesses in our IT systems and processes? What does our external auditor say about them?

- Do we have adequate plans in place to manage a crisis caused by a cyberincident? Is management regularly exercising the plans?

- Are we investing enough to ensure that our IT systems are not easy targets?

- Where do management and our security teams disagree on cyber security? With what outcomes?

Finally, it is important to remember that risks also provide opportunities. Could your business generate more revenue and profit by upgrading your IT systems to make them more secure?

6. Ensure that the risks are properly managed through an enterprise-wide framework, with adequate staffing and budget.

Many companies operate through a series of silos, with individual departments and business units making independent decisions. This is a really dangerous practice when it comes to cyber security, because digital technology takes no account of boundaries and silos.

Your Board should ensure that your management tackles this weakness. The first step is to appoint a cross-organisational cyber risk management team.

The team should comprise senior representatives of all major stakeholder departments.[6] A senior manager with cross-departmental authority should lead the team. This could be the CFO, CRO or COO, for example – but it should not be the CIO, to make clear that cyber-security is not just an IT issue.

The senior executive in charge should ensure that his team meets regularly and develops:

- *Reports for the Board* with metrics that quantify the business impact of the cyber risk. The Internal Audit function should audit the effectiveness of cyber risk management as part of their quarterly review process;

---

6. Business Units, Legal, Internal Audit and Compliance (IAC), Finance, HR, IT, Communications and Risk Management.

- *Plans for cyber risk management and communications* across all departments and business units. All stakeholders need to be involved in developing this plan and to feel ownership of it;

- *An adequate total cyber risk budget* that recognises the resource implications across the business and ensures that the budget for cyber security is not exclusively focussed on IT; and

- *Confidence* that management systematically identifies how to manage different types of cyber risk.

As with any other area of enterprise risk, your company should align its risk appetite and investment strategy. This will also help you to identify the level of cyber risk your organisation needs to accept as a practical business consideration.

Once again, you need a detailed discussion with your management to ensure that they are addressing the following issues:

- We know that we are going to suffer a successful cyber-attack. When it happens, what loss of data can we accept?

- When it comes to mitigation, what is the correct balance in investment between basic defences and the advanced security needed to protect our "crown jewels"?

This should be a self-evident distinction, but in practice many organisations apply security controls equally across all IT data. This does not make economic sense; protecting low-impact systems and data from the most sophisticated threats will require greater investment than the benefits warrant. Your management should consider giving only minimal protection to low probability/low-impact risks.

- How should we assess the impact of cyber events?

This can be more complicated than it appears. An obvious example is that publicity about cyber breaches often makes a purely logical risk management response impossible. External stakeholders may see little difference between a small and a large or dangerous breach. This could mean that damage to your corporate reputation and even your share price may not correspond directly to the importance of the event. In other words, traditional risk management approaches to assessing damage based on potential impact may not apply in a cyber context.

When it comes to the transfer of risk, there is now an increasing range of insurance solutions available. They will include cover for financial loss, but also help in mitigating the risk of property damage and physical injury resulting from a cyber breach.

Some insurers now also offer access to pro-active tools, employee training, IT security advice and expert response services.

The inclusion of these value-added services further demonstrates the importance of moving cyber security outside the IT department and more into the Executive Committee and the Boardroom.

8. Know the law: you need to understand the legal and regulatory implications of cyber risk.

Successful cyber-attacks may lead to litigation and even to a personal liability for directors and senior executives.

Your Legal Counsel will provide you with a detailed briefing, but a salutary warning of the risks comes with the implementation in May 2018 of the European Union's General Data Protection Regulation (GDPR). This opens a significant regulatory risk for any organisation managing the data of EU citizens, even from outside the EU.

To demonstrate that your Board takes its legal and regulatory responsibilities seriously, it needs to carefully minute your regular discussions of cyber risk. The minutes should show that your directors have made informed decisions in your oversight of the company's cyber-security strategy.

You also need to be clear about what information your organisation must disclose when it suffers a successful cyber-attack.

CONCLUSION

Cyber security is one of the most urgent and serious enterprise risk issues to face your business. It is certainly much more than a purely technical and operational IT issue that only nerds can understand.

Your Board needs to develop its ability to address cyber risk, both as part of your duty as directors, and as part of your oversight of your management.

2.2 ACTIVATING THE HUMAN FIREWALL: THE LEAP FROM KNOWING TO DOING

Mike Carter and Amanda Price, Creative Directors at Layer 8 Ltd

"Annual e-learning will not instil and sustain the cyber resilient behaviours that employees need today. We're trying to 'programme' our people in the same way we programme computers: to do certain things, in defined ways at certain times. This approach doesn't work with people."[1]

In 2016's *Managing Cybersecurity Risk*, Nick Wilding of AXELOS Global Best Practice wrote about the serious limitations of traditional 'one size fits all' compliance-based approaches to educating staff about cybersecurity, and posited a new approach that places people centre stage. Such an approach, he argued, is vital if all-important security behaviours are to be adopted and embedded across a business.

It's an irony that for all our technological advancement we haven't yet mastered the behaviours we need to keep us secure, nor worked out how best to train and educate our employees as frontline defenders of their organisation. A common complaint is that employees know what to do but they just don't do it. Awareness of rules and best practice consistently fails to produce effective follow-through when it comes to security behaviours, whether it's exercising caution around emails, locking screens when leaving computers unattended, or shredding documents before they go to recycling. This leap, from knowing what the right thing to do is, to doing the right thing consistently, is like the Holy Grail for security professionals. How to close this gap is what we are concerned with in this chapter.

It's easy to state the problems the 'human factor' presents for business but there have been relatively few attempts to understand the context which perpetuates non-

---

1. Wilding, Nick, 'Turning Your People into Your Most Effective Defence: A Different Approach' in *Managing Cybersecurity Risk 2016*, Legend Business

compliant behaviours[2] and the cultural constraints thwarting a proactive approach to security practices.[3] In this chapter we begin by considering some 'blockers' to widescale adoption of security behaviours, and then explore the use of conversation, core values and collaboration as a framework for developing a proactive security culture founded on responsible action. Finally, we offer some practical suggestions for making the leap from awareness to behaviours.

WHAT DO WE WANT AND WHY DON'T WE HAVE IT?

In 2017, data breach surveys[4] consistently cited employees as the cause of over 90% of data breaches. The most common causes of breach are:

- Clicking on malicious links;

- Downloading malicious files;

- Loss of data due to error or theft; and

- Unauthorised entry to data or premises.

It is clear that human vulnerability is now the cybercriminal's target of choice. The spectrum of potential for individuals causing a breach in the workplace is growing incrementally, and will increase dramatically as the 'Internet of Things' turns the business environment into a 'smart' space. To date, businesses have depended on annual security awareness courses, computer-based training modules, policy emailed out to employees, and maybe the odd video, but we know these solutions have no long-term effect because employees continue to make the same mistakes.

Traditional security awareness is founded on the attempt to prevent security breaches from happening with a rule-based approach that is essentially reactive and top-down, and which provides only the most basic knowledge for members of the workforce. Intensive training on one type of phishing email or ransomware link, can be rapidly made redundant by a shift in tactics on the part of the cybercriminals. Such attempts at prevention create a 'cat-and-mouse' game which the criminal will always win.

---

2. There are exceptions, of course. See, for example: Kirlappos, I., Beautement, A., Sasse, MA., '*"Comply or Die" Is Dead: Long live security-aware principal agents'*, 2013, UCL, PDF accessed at: http://discovery.ucl. ac.uk/1419506/1/Kirlappos-Comply%20or%20Die.pdf

3. Lance Spitzner writes often on this in his SANS Security Awareness Blog, accessed at: https://securingthehuman. sans.org/blog

4. See, for example: BakerHostetler's *Data Security Incident Response Report 2017*, *Cyber Security Breaches Survey 2017*, and the 2017 *Data Breach Investigations Report* by Verizon.

TRAINING FOR PROACTIVE FRONTLINE DEFENDERS

Compliance-based training modules tend to test short-term retention of knowledge and little more; a workforce that is *talking* about security is starting to take long-term responsibility for it. Many businesses are now moving beyond compliance towards a more dynamic framework in which employees and the executive work together to learn how best to secure their assets. According to Erlend Andreas Gjære[5], instead of complex annual training schedules and compliance testing, this approach requires two fundamental elements:

- That people are able and willing to report.

- That the organisation is willing to learn.

These two conditions provide a cultural context of mutual benefit based on trust and responsibility, in place of blame and culpability. To be prepared for the ever-evolving 21st century threat landscape, organisations must be engaged in an ongoing conversation about security that reaches from the board to the sub-contracted cleaning staff, they must recognise that collaborative action based on shared information is fundamental, and they must be secure by design rather than policy-dependent.

Learning to learn together leads us out of the age of the PowerPoint presentation, towards a consideration of culture as the starting point for secure behaviours.

WHAT'S NEEDED TO GET THE BEHAVIOURS WE DESIRE?

"Security is not a technology challenge. If it were, technology would have fixed the problems a long time ago. Security is a people challenge, a social and organisational challenge. It's a cultural challenge."[6]

Security awareness is necessary to stimulate the potential for behavioural change, but a conducive culture is essential for behavioural change to happen and to embed itself. Culture is, by its nature, about people – and it is vital to the success of any people-centred security strategy. Businesses who place their trust in tech and tech alone will produce a workforce who simply do not believe that security is their responsibility.

A simple and useful definition of security culture is how we collectively demonstrate

---

5. Gjære, Erlend Andreas, 'Four Steps to Have Employees Report Security Incidents (And Save the Day)', 2017, Security & People, accessed at: https://securityandpeople.com/2017/08/four-steps-to-have-employees-report-security-incidents/

6 Hayden, Lance, 'People-Centric Security: Transforming Your Enterprise Security Culture', 2015, McGraw-Hill Education, p 10

what matters to us on a daily basis through what we say and what we do. So, culture is about behaviours, yes, but it's also about conversations. When, every day, across an organisation, people are talking about security and doing things to improve it, that is security culture. And if people aren't talking about it, or they're talking about it negatively and behaving in ways that put their company at risk, then that is still security culture – just not a desirable one.

Bolt-on security procedures which slow down an employee's ability to work effectively and efficiently will create antipathy towards security and IT professionals, leading to security workarounds with the potential to harm the business – and a 'shadow' security culture is born.[7] So security culture, it seems, is what happens when the CISO isn't looking, and until businesses tackle security culturally, the established and prevailing culture of the business will trump strategy every time.

Let's look at a simple example of this in action. Somebody gets up from their desk to go and make a cup of coffee. Halfway to the kitchen they realise they've left their screen unlocked and they pause. Only last week they took the annual security e-learning course, so they know why locking their screen is important. Then they see all the other unlocked screens and go and make that coffee. Those unlocked screens speak louder than e-learning about what the business really believes.

It works the other way, too: when a majority of locked screens signals the importance of the behaviour – backed up by conversations when people forget to lock them – then there is a cultural pressure being applied to support awareness and behaviour. In this example, it matters to the employee what their peers think of them. That may be the only reason why they enact the secure behaviour but at least the behaviour is correct. However, there is a deeper determinant of behaviour that can be culturally communicated and it's essential in any people-centred security strategy: values.

If security culture is how we collectively demonstrate what matters to us on a daily basis through what we say and what we do, then culture speaks of our values. In an organisation where there is a poor security culture there is every likelihood that people are not emotionally engaged or in touch with the things that they and the business care about. Security culture change involves shining a light on the value system employees and the wider organisation share.

Who doesn't want to be seen as trustworthy, caring and willing to go the extra mile to protect the business? Who doesn't want to be seen as conscientious, fiercely loyal to their colleagues and a safe pair of hands? It's difficult to read these questions without an emotional response and the desire to assimilate those defining characteristics into

---

7 Kirlappos, I., Parkin, S., Sasse, MA., *Learning from "Shadow Security:" Why Understanding Non-Compliance Provides the Basis for Effective Security* 2014, UCL, PDF accessed at: http://discovery.ucl.ac.uk/1424472/1/Kirlappos%20et%20al.%20-%202014%20-%20Learning%20from%20%E2%80%9CShadow%20Security%E2%80%9D%20Why%20understanding.pdf

our self-image is a powerful driver to behaviour. When they are invoked and directly attached to desired security behaviours – and they are ideas that are alive in the culture – then security becomes a very personal matter. Employees want to go home at the end of the day satisfied at having done a good day's work – and they want to pride themselves on having protected customers, colleagues and their business against criminals.

HOW DO YOU DO SECURITY CULTURE CHANGE?

"The reality is that today's security pros need to go beyond technical expertise. Security practitioners need to be good communicators who can connect cybersecurity issues to business priorities, rally the rest of the organisation to get involved, solve tough problems and handle sensitive issues with integrity."[8]

The role of the security professional has evolved rapidly over the past decade to encompass leadership, communication, and strategy. It's no longer unusual for security roles to be filled by people with relatively little technical experience but with a detailed understanding of communications, marketing and behavioural psychology.

At the heart of every effective security culture change programme is the initiation of a conversation about security which stretches from the boardroom to the basement. If employees don't talk about security, they won't behave securely – and if employees don't behave securely, they won't be effective defenders of the organisation, no matter how many training sessions they attend.

GETTING THE CONVERSATION STARTED

Conversations happen all the time, everywhere, in every business – they're fluid, improvisational and dynamic. Whether they arrive in an inbox, start over coffee, or form the centrepiece of a team meeting, conversations about security need to be informative *and* have relevance for the people involved.

Here's a list of 'golden rules' we've developed for getting people engaged in the security conversation:

Explain Why – Once we know *why* we're being asked to behave in a certain way, we are more likely to make the necessary change.

Make it Human – Protecting abstract data elicits no emotional response, protecting people's identities does.

---

8 Erlin, Tim, 'The need for soft skills in cybersecurity has increased, says Tripwire Inc', 2017, Vanilla Plus, accessed at https://www.vanillaplus.com/2017/10/18/31531-need-soft-skills-cybersecurity-increased-says-tripwire-inc/

Create Conundrums – Instead of *telling* people what to do, give them a complex scenario and *ask* them: "What would you do?"

Ignite Lively Debates – Get employees to share tips on hot topics like secure browsing for young people.

Recognise Proactive Behaviour – Invite nominations for an 'unsung security hero'. Share the hero's story, their passion for security and their advice to others.

Make it Current – Post or talk about big breaches that hit the headlines. Share your own thoughts and comments on them.

Create Events – Generate a buzz around something, and why not have Security Awareness Month every month instead of once a year?

Fun is Allowed – Run a competition to find the best security-themed joke, poem or YouTube video.

CONVERSATION IN ACTION

Conversations change culture – but culture, as we have noted, is more than talking; it has responsible action at its heart. So how do we demonstrate to the employees who populate our businesses and organisations what we mean by this? What kind of training leads to behavioural change?

Experiential training is, by its very nature, engaging. It's an opportunity for debate and for deep learning. Participants leave an effective session feeling motivated, energised and confident in their ability to defend their businesses and their homes. The effects are long-lasting and they fuel ongoing conversations that, in turn, strengthen the developing culture. Interactive events could be as simple as asking everyone to provide a security tip at the beginning of a meeting, or as complex as a one-day, professionally-run, immersive crisis response workshop.

Here's an example of experiential learning we've used many times. It's simple to set up, can be run in as little as 30 minutes and is really enjoyable for participants.

The Hacker's Perspective
Employees take on the role of the villain and, working in small teams, plan an attack on their own business. Everyone is given permission to wreak havoc – on paper – and there might even be the promise of a prize to the best 'hack'. Once the judging is complete, the employees consider what actions they could take to stop their hacks happening for real.

There are real and lasting benefits of this workshop:

- The mixture of 'dare' and 'challenge' brings the kind of focus and energy to cybersecurity that security professionals dream of.

- Participants discover what they *don't* know, such as what data is valuable to a hacker and why. This leads to questions, sharing of knowledge, and fevered internet searches.

- Vulnerabilities start to make sense. The 'hackers' are able to look at themselves as end-users from a different perspective and begin to understand why certain behaviours are so dangerous.

- Once there's a villain, heroes are born, giving the role of 'frontline defender' new weight and moral integrity.

- Playful hackers are a security professional's best friend. Planning an attack gives clarity of vision; the 'villain' can critique the business with a professional eye and provide clear feedback on what needs to be sharpened up.

We've run this activity numerous times with large and small businesses and it never fails, so long as it's playful, fun and not about 'teaching'. Involving participants in workshops, setting them tasks, requiring them to take the lead, enabling them to set their own agenda for action after the workshop – these are huge strides towards a proactive culture of security. It has to be this way: our culture belongs to everyone and culture change is by its very nature inclusive.

Collaborative Policy Making
Workshops such as 'The Hacker's Perspective' should culminate with participants identifying a series of behaviours and committing to implementing them. The behaviours can be very simple and people may express relief that there is a clear way for them to demonstrate that they care about security. Change is already happening.

A list of behaviours arrived at in this way can form the basis of a departmental best practice document or team charter, but it's also possible to take this a stage further and develop policy with the input of the people who will have to follow it. Policies should be living, breathing documents that can be understood quickly and easily, and provide immediate practical guidance to the reader. Employees will more readily buy in to a policy they have helped to create and that they have tailored to their particular needs.

SPREADING THE CONVERSATION

If security culture is a conversation that includes everyone, then how can security professionals make that happen?

It begins with the willingness of the board to trust and learn from their employees and the creation of a network of 'Security Champions' or 'Security Advocates'. These are people working in all areas and at all levels of the organisation who take on the role of leading and educating others as part of their existing job. They take the security conversation out into the business and make it their mission to communicate key messages, demonstrate good practice and show the importance of taking the initiative when they spot something that isn't right.

Because of their local knowledge of people and processes they are able to be focused in their approach, determine priorities and tailor what they do to the needs of their particular area or department. And, because they have established relationships with colleagues, their advice will be respected and acted upon immediately. They enable changes in behaviour to be measured by assessing what's actually happening and reporting back on risks and vulnerabilities, as well as improvements and good practice. They are well placed to congratulate colleagues and offer encouragement.

An effective security culture change campaign will culminate in every single employee seeing themselves as a 'member of the security team'.

A STRATEGY FOR SECURITY CULTURE CHANGE

Every organisation is learning how to best secure their assets in an ever-evolving threat landscape. Engaging every single employee in that process is crucial to creating integrated, effective and proactive defences. The organisations that learn quickest how to best defend themselves, are those which are prepared to learn together, make learning co-dependent, and recognise the importance of a fully active 'human firewall'.

We have presented, in outline, a coherent strategy for meeting the challenge of the human factor in security. Awareness, behaviours and culture are the 'ABC' of components necessary for change; conversations and communications, interactive training workshops that demand action, and peer-to-peer learning and leadership via a 'champions' campaign are, together, the means to make it happen. They work in concert and complement each other.

Security culture change is not a monolithic phenomenon – it can't happen all at once and there is no silver bullet – it happens one conversation and one behaviour at a time. But it can spread and develop exponentially until a tipping point is reached and nothing short of transformation occurs. People *are* the solution: they want to be a safe pair of hands and they want to protect the people and things that matter to them.

2.3 THE RESILIENT ORGANISATION – ARE WE SEARCHING FOR OUR "PHLOGISTON"?

Kev Brear and Vijay Rathour

INTRODUCTION

Cyber resilience is still a new and emerging concept, but there is a wealth of relevant and potentially applicable academic research into the subject of organisational resilience available from the business management and administration arena that may be instructive in this rapidly evolving space. It is believed that the existing research into organisational resilience may be leveraged to assist in the evolution and development of cyber resilience. This article is designed to highlight the connectivity across the academic disciplines and to assist in the evolution and development processes.

Over the past decade, a number of academics and industry professionals from the field of risk have published articles or comments on the subject of organisational resilience (Somers, 2009, Crichton, et al, 2009 and Auerswald, 2006). Industry standards have also been published on the subject, such as BS 65000:2014 *Guidance on Organizational Resilience*, ISO 22316:2017 *Security and Resilience – Organizational Resilience* and *ASIS SPC.1-2009: Organizational Resilience: Security, Preparedness and Continuity Management Systems - Requirements with Guidance for Use* from the United States of America. Of the three standards referenced, this latter standard is perhaps the most interesting, and possibly controversial, as it sets out a list of requirements or activities to be performed by the adopters that should then achieve the outcome of a "resilient organisation".

Cyber security is commonly being considered one of the priorities for businesses in the United Kingdom[1]. The concept of "resilience" is now being actively considered in the context and world of cyber risks facing every connected business and individual.

---

1. Allianz Risk Barometer

Added to this, the notion that a technology environment can ever be made secure against all impending risks, such as attack, error or failure, has generally been accepted as unachievable. The current view espoused by many industry observers is that the range of cyber risks, threats and attack vectors is so wide, dynamic and evolving that the only real option is to plan to face the challenges that these adverse events will create for organisations and society. However, the maturity of resilience in the context of cyber related risks has not yet achieved the same level of maturity as that in relation to organisational resilience. The first standard on the subject of cyber resilience is due to be published in 2018 by the British Standards Institute, entitled *BS 31111 Cyber Risk and Resilience*. It is envisaged that this standard will provide high-level guidance and good practice signposts to the senior managers and leaders of organisations.

BACKGROUND

The positions on organisational resilience voiced by the various commentators and the particular standards mentioned mainly concern themselves with what actually constitutes organisational resilience. In the case of Somers (2009), a proposal is made as to how levels of organisational resilience could possibly be measured in some organisations.

Phlogiston theory was first espoused by Johann Joachim Becher in his 1667 treatise, *Physical Education*. Becher stated that phlogiston was a colourless, odourless, weightless material without mass that was present in all combustible material and that could only be released by combustion. It was also described as "anti-oxygen" by some scientists of the time. After Belcher's work was published, many of his peers and followers supported the theory and expounded considerable amounts of time and resources on working to prove the existence of the element and the accuracy of the theory. The theory of the existence of phlogiston persisted for about 100 years, until it was thoroughly discredited through the results of empirical research by the French scientist Antoine-Laurent Lavoisier.

Reviewing organisational resilience, this chapter discusses:

- The relationship between this theory and the theory of the firm or organisation and examines some of the issues that may be revealed in that relationship by Senge (2006) and Grey (2005);

- Whether there is a paradox between the theory of organisational resilience and contingency theory from the field of management research;

- The relationship between organisational resilience and risk management, with particular focus upon the relationship with the concept of Enterprise Risk

Management and building networks that can adapt to the changing pictures of risk (Apgar, 2006); and

- Emerging trends in the theory of organisational resilience and will endeavour to assist the reader to reach a considered conclusion on the question posed by the title.

ORGANISATIONAL RESILIENCE

The first issue that must be examined is the definition of organisational resilience and this is where one may encounter the first problem with the theory. As Somers (2009) reports, there has been a considerable amount of research into the management of organisations and a further amount of debate about what actually constitutes resilience within an organisational context, but there has been little research into what constitutes a resilient organisation.

There may be a multitude of reasons for this apparent void, but one explanation may be drawn from the lessons identified from the publication of *In Search of Excellence: lessons from America's best run companies*, published by Peters and Waterman in 1982. Peters and Waterman published the results of their research into the organisational structures of a number of American firms and corporations. Peters and Waterman concluded that 43 of the organisations researched were "successful" and they further identified and measured 8 areas of organisational activity, which they then claimed had contributed to these organisations' "excellence".

By 1984, the assertions of Peters and Waterman were challenged, as several of the 43 organisations had encountered difficulties because of financial problems or apparent management errors and mistakes. As a result, some of the 43 "excellent" organisations had actually ceased to exist (Grey 2005:67). This example encapsulates one issue at the heart of organisational resilience: the concept is a snapshot in time and at the moment the organisation is assessed it may be resilient, but that assessment does not then guarantee or provide any assurances about the future performance of the organisation in the area of organisational resilience and it has also been suggested that the wholesale adoption of the elements that make one organisation resilient may not be effective or sufficient in another organisation (La Porte, 2006:73).

This problem is exacerbated by the issue that there is considerable debate about what constitutes an organisation and numerous theories about organisations by such notable commentators as Weber, Taylor, Maslow, Herzberg, Senge and many others who lead the researcher to the rather uncomfortable conclusion that there is a multitude of theories on the subject, all of which were logical to their developers, all of which had validity within the context of their supporting research, all with academic rigour and all have contributed to the body of knowledge on the subject (Grey 2005, Weick 2009).

However, Senge (2006: 267-71) also states that he believes that most of the existing theories or thought processes around organisations and their structures are flawed and that organisations should be viewed as open ended systems that are living entities. This type of thinking is reflected by Turner & Pidgeon (1997) and Toft and Reynolds (2005), who employ the terms socio-technical or socio-technological systems to describe environments that may also be termed by some as organisations, where humans and technology interact, but conversely may also be viewed as component parts of larger entities or collections.

This type of approach to the issue is very relevant when considering the theories of Weick (2009) and Reason (2007), who employ the term "High Reliability Organizations" or Perrow, who employs the term "High Reliability Theory" (1999: 372) and then utilises hospital emergency departments, forest fire-fighting teams, aircraft carriers in the US Navy, nuclear power plants and chemical production plants, as examples of the type of organisations that can deliver resilience or high reliability. Using Grey (2005)'s logic these examples could all be seen as organisations in their own right, but equally they may also be viewed as sub-sectors or divisions within much larger organisations.

The issue of resilience in organisations is also commented upon by Pugh and Hickson (2007: 153), who quote Crozier and his conclusions on French organisations that were exhibiting the profound characteristics of a bureaucratic structure:

"It is an alternation of long periods of stability with very short periods of crisis and change. Conflicts are stifled until they explode. Explosive crises are therefore endemic to such bureaucracies, and necessary to them as a means for change."

Crozier's view was that crises stimulate change and so were therefore a necessity in some types of organisational structure for the continued evolution of the organisation. This conclusion is aligned to contingency theory, which states that organisations change shape, management styles and structure in reaction to the changes (whether social, natural, economic, political or technical) in the environments in which they operate. Crozier's conclusions were originally published in 1964 and were drawn from his research into organisations and management. However, Crozier also stated that such crises often led to an individual emerging from the ranks of the afflicted organisation to lead the way out of the period of adversity. Crozier does not reflect on the potential scenario where such an individual is not found to face the challenges.

RISK

Having raised the subject of risk, it would seem appropriate to review the relationships between organisational resilience and risk management. The review process may be somewhat challenging because risk and its management is another very contentious discipline that has evolved from mainly constructionist perspectives for the qualitative approach and mainly positivist perspectives for the quantitative approach to risk.

This method of evolution has led to some rather controversial scenarios: for example Taleb's *The Black Swan* (2007), in which he sets out the convincing case that the quantitative approach to risk assessments within organisational contexts is inadequate and he goes on to propose his "own" approach to the issue of risk management in organisations. At this point, it is probably right and proper to highlight that Taleb's academic discipline or background is Mathematics and so his skill is undoubted in terms of quantitative risk assessment. However, the suggested "new" approach to risk management that Taleb advocates is actually a classic example of a qualitative approach to risk assessment and management, that should be instantly recognisable to any students of the works of Hood & Jones (2002), Lagadec (1993), Apgar (2006), Perry & Quarantelli (2005) and Daniels, et al, (2006) to name but a few, who have published work in that arena.

The US standard (2009) on organisational resilience took a risk based approach to the issue and proposed that organisations implemented a management system that drew together the various elements or sections of the organisation into a concerted effort of holistic protection. The main issue with this approach is that the standard requires the organisation to first identify those sections or sectors that require risk management structures to be constructed for the protection of their respective operations and to leave out of scope those parts of the organisation that do not require those considerations. The flaw in this logic is quite apparent, as it is known from historical evidence that any risk assessment process may be flawed, and so the potential to omit a section of the organisation that then ferments a crisis or disaster for the organisation within it is quite evident.

The writers of the organisational resilience standard could counter that issue by stating that both crisis management and business continuity arrangements could be put in place within an organisation to counter that potential scenario. However, it could be suggested that the logic is exactly the same as saying that a society can deal with the risk of crime taking place in its cities by deploying an effective police service. Now is not the time or place to discuss criminology, but it may be fair to suggest that deployment of a police service may only reduce the risk of a crime occurring and may only increase slightly the chance of a perpetrator being located for the offence.

If it is accepted that resilience within an organisation is a risk management issue, then the question may arise: should resilience of the organisation be part of an enterprise risk management structure or is organisational resilience another term for what has been viewed previously as enterprise risk management? In 2004, Enterprise Risk Management was defined by the Committee of the Sponsoring Organizations of the Treadway Commission as:

"… a process, effected by an entity's board of directors, management and other personnel, applied in strategy setting and across the enterprise, designed to identify potential events that may affect the entity, and manage risk to be within its risk appetite, to provide reasonable assurance regarding the achievement of entity objectives."

Having obtained that definition it may now be appropriate to set out the definition of Organizational Resilience Management, contained within the 2009 US standard on that topic, which states that:

"Organizational Resilience (OR) Management: systemic and coordinated activities and practices through which an organization manages its operational risks and the associated potential threats and impacts therein."

And it further states that:

"Organizational Resilience (OR) management program: Ongoing management and governance process supported by top management, resourced to ensure that the necessary steps are taken to identify the impact of potential losses; maintain viable recovery strategies and plans; and ensure continuity of functions / products / services through exercising, rehearsal, testing, training, maintenance and assurance."

When the two elements of the organisational resilience definition are co-joined it has to be said that there appears to be very little difference in strategic objectives between the organisational resilience definitions provided in the US standard and the COSO definition of enterprise risk management provided. At this point, it should also be reported that the definition of organisational resilience in the US standard may produce similar outcomes, in an organisational context, to the definition provided for Business Continuity in the BSI standard BS25999:1 (2006), which stated:

"Holistic management process that identifies potential threats to an organization and the impacts to business operations that those threats, if realized, might cause, and which provides a framework for building organizational resilience with the capability for an effective response that safeguards the interests of its key stakeholders, reputation, brand and value-creating activities.

*   NOTE: Business continuity management involves managing the recovery or continuation of business activities in the event of a business disruption, and management of the overall programme through training, exercises and reviews, to ensure the business continuity plan(s) stays current and up-to-date."*

Lastly, on the subject of risk management within an organisational context, Apgar (2006) sets out the case for deploying a qualitative risk management system within an organisation and Apgar employs similar justification, with similar supporting examples, for that approach as Taleb (2007) employs in his publication.

CONCLUSIONS

This chapter set out to discuss the concept of organisational resilience and establish if such a state of existence may be desirable within an organisation. The chapter has established that resilience within an organisation's operations may provide benefits and it has further established that there are a number of theories and methodologies that are currently in circulation, which claim that their adoption by an organisation may produce an outcome of a more resilient organization.

Cyber related risks are just one of the risk areas that should be considered in the context of the wider enterprise risk management arena to develop a more strategic and coherent approach to the challenges involved. To support that position, it has been shown that risk management activities within an organisation should be placed within the framework of an appropriate management system, but it is suggested that it is for the particular organisation to adopt the most suitable type of framework for its activities that will enable it to most effectively meet its strategic objectives.

It has also been shown that organisational resilience and a resilient organisation are two very different concepts and that attainment of the first state may not necessarily lead to the second state for any one particular organisation or any element or sub division within an organisation.

REFERENCES

Apgar, D., (2006). *Risk Intelligence, Learning to manage what we don't know*, Boston: Harvard Business School Publishing.

ASIS SPC.1-2009: Organizational Resilience: Security, Preparedness and Continuity Management Systems - Requirements with Guidance for Use, Alexandria: ASIS / American National Standards Institute, Inc.

Auerswald, P.E., Branscomb, L.M., La Porte, T.M., Michel-Kerjan, E.O., (2006). *Seeds of Disaster, Roots of Response: How private action can reduce public vulnerability*, New York: Cambridge University Press.

Britannia Online Encyclopaedia, *Phlogiston Chemical Theory* (available at http://www.britannica.com/EBchecked/topic/456974/phlogiston), accessed on 04/09/09.

British Standards Institute. (2006). *BS 25999-1: 2006 Business Continuity Management Part 1: Code of Practice*, London: British Standards Institute.

Crichton, M.T., Ramsay, C.G., Kelly, T., (2009). *Enhancing Organisational Resilience through Emergency Planning: Learnings from Cross-sectoral Lessons* in *Journal of Contingencies and Crisis Management,* (Volume 16, Number 4, December 2008, pp: 24-37) Oxford: Blackwell Publishing Ltd.

Daniels, R.J., Kettl, D.F., Kunreuther, H., (2006). *On Risk and Disaster, Lessons from Hurricane Katrina,* Philadelphia: University of Pennsylvania Press.

Enterprise Risk Management – Integrated Framework, Executive Summary (2004), USA: Committee of Sponsoring Organizations of the Treadway Commission (COSO).

Fink, S., (2002). *Crisis Management, planning for the inevitable,* Lincoln: iUniverse Inc.

Grey, C., (2005). *A very short, fairly interesting and reasonably cheap book about studying organizations,* London: Sage Publications Ltd.

Hood, C. & Jones, D. ed., (2002). *Accident and Design,* London: Routledge.

Hood, C., Jones, J., Pidgeon, N. & Turner, B., (1992). *Risk Analysis, Perception & Management,* London: The Royal Society.

Lagadec, P., (1993). *Preventing Chaos in a Crisis,* London: McGraw-Hill Book Company.

Mitroff, I., (2005). *Why some companies emerge better and stronger from a crisis,* New York: AMACOM.

Perrow, C., (1999). *Normal Accidents, Living with High-risk technologies,* Princeton: Princeton University Press.

Perry, R.W., Quarantelli, E.L., (2005). *What is a Disaster? New answers to old questions,* USA: Xlibris Corporation.

Pugh, D.S., Hickson, D.J., (2007). *Writers on Organizations,* 6th Ed., London: The Penguin Group.

Reason, J., (2007). *Human Error,* 18th printing. New York: Cambridge University Press.

Reason, J., (2008). *Managing the risks of organisational accidents*, Aldershot: Ashgate Publishing Company.

Senge, P., (2006). *The Fifth Discipline*, London: Random House Business Books.

Somers, S., (2009). *Measuring Resilience Potential: an Adaptive Strategy for Organizational Crisis Planning* in *Journal of Contingencies and Crisis Management*, (Volume 16, Number 4, December 2008, pp: 24-37) Oxford: Blackwell Publishing Ltd.

Taleb, N.N., (2007). *The Black Swan*, London: The Penguin Group.

Toft, B., Reynolds, S., (2005). *Learning from Disasters*, 3rd ed. Basingstoke: Perpetuity Press Limited / Palgrave Macmillan.

Turner, B.A., Pidgeon, N.F., (1997). *Man-Made Disasters*, 2nd ed. Oxford: Butterworth-Heinemann.

Weick, K.E., (2009). *Making Sense of the Organization Volume 2, The Impermanent Organization*, Chichester: John Wiley & Sons

2.4 IF A BREACH HAPPENS – AN ACTION PLAN FOR RESPONSE AND DAMAGE CONTAINMENT

Alexander Ellrodt, Deutsche Bank

Cyber threats have become key business risks. They are no longer just IT issues and are a fundamental problem in a digitalised world. Cyber security is a well-established discipline trying to prevent a breach. However, any organisation needs to get ready to respond if such a breach happens, regardless of how well the company has protected its information and IT. It is therefore necessary for organisations to develop and establish a response plan to deal with cyber related issues.

CYBER INCIDENT RESPONSE PLAN (IRP)

A cyber incident response plan or breach plan is an essential tool to manage a cyber breach and its consequences. In this chapter we will take a closer look at the IRP components and how to practise them effectively. When we talk about incidents or breaches it is important to understand what exactly has happened, i.e. has been breached. For example it will be quite relevant to understand if data has been stolen, manipulated, deleted or encrypted. If data is impacted you must make sure you understand the data category, i.e. is it personal data, business critical data or other regulated data? Failure to understand data is likely to result in reputational and financial consequences post incident. Also, it is vital to understand if the incident has concluded or if it is still in progress. If an incident is still ongoing it might be more relevant to deal with countermeasures and containment then data restoration. The IRP is designed to manage breaches of data, systems and networks. This list is not exclusive as the IRP should contain all relevant components based on the design of business process, IT and other relevant factors. IRPs are multifaceted which makes it difficult to determine all relevant considerations. A good IRP should therefore involve all relevant parties and stakeholders to ensure all factors have been considered. It is very similar to a Business Continuity Plan but with a specific focus on cyber incidents.

IRP TEAM

The IRP must be written, maintained and executed by a team, the IRP team. The IRP team has to collect the relevant data points from the stakeholders which makes the building of the IRP a collaborative effort across the organisation. It is therefore very important to ensure good and complete documentation enriched by training and exercises which should also lead to updates of the IRP. Do not just download a template and complete it. Every organisation is different and the IRP as well as the team needs to be customised to allow the organisation to respond effectively. Many experienced IRP teams continue to develop their plans and exercises constantly.

For larger organisations it is advisable to establish priorities like client information, financially sensitive or private data and staff safety. The size of the team depends on the complexity of the organisation as well as the size and the impact of the breach. As a general rule the team should comprise the following roles and departments:

- The team leader

- The incident/breach manager

- Legal counsel

- Human Resources

- Operations/Business

- Communications/Public Relations (internal/external)

The IRP team's main tasks are to manage the incident itself, communicate up and internally as well as activating response, business continuity and disaster recovery plans as required.

The cyber response itself should be covered by a team of experts. Such experts can be either maintained in-house, on-boarded at short notice or a combination of both. Many smaller sized companies cannot afford to maintain a whole team of cyber defence experts. Such companies often hire external specialists in advance or contract with expert firms to allow a timely and professional response to cyber-attacks once needed. The agreed response times for individual experts or specialised providers are of utmost importance as the cyber-attack will not wait for any response team or consultant to arrive. Contracts must include response time clauses and such response times should be trained and exercised annually, at least

DEFINING KEY ASSETS AND THREATS

A good IRP identifies the key IT and Information Security assets up front or uses existing repositories to assess threats and risks. This will also allow the identification of security measures and protection levels. Assets range from data, network, LAN/WLAN and to document classifications. The threats form scenarios for the IRP team to plan against and to practise. These typically are worms, malware, system failures, intrusion, denial-of-service, internal abuse or spyware.

IDENTIFYING THE BREACH/ATTACK

In order to respond appropriately it is important to understand the scope, extent and type of attack or incident. To do so a monitoring program must be established. In its simplest form such monitoring should be built based on two components – technical monitoring, for example a network intrusion system, and issue monitoring, for example an employee reporting a customer complaint or strange behaviour of IT systems. Both can be outsourced if a permanent team is too costly. However, notifying a third party provider should be defined, rehearsed and relatively easy to do, especially for non-IT staff. An internal IRP team is still required to steer the response but the expert knowledge to respond technically can be sourced from outside the company. In this context it is advisable to establish a severity rating matrix or similar classification logic. This will also help to determine if the breach requires a Crisis Management activation and response.

When a breach happens or has happened there are a number of mandatory actions to be taken. These actions should be documented in a checklist or aide memoire. It is best to work down the list once the team has been assembled and is ready to respond. The key actions include:

- Recording the incident from the time of breach until the response and follow up has concluded;

- Activating the IRP team and all outside response and support individuals;

- Informing relevant stakeholders both inside and outside the organisation,including third party vendors (following approval by accountable executives);

- Taking operational, tactical and strategic decisions; and

- Responding to the attack or breach with the appropriate countermeasures.

ACTIVATING THE IRP AND TEAM

IRP teams do not assemble themselves automatically. A good response can only be managed if an ongoing monitoring and alarm process is in place. For the technical aspects of Cyber security, many organisations have a 24/7 security monitoring in place. Smaller organisations often have external service providers monitoring their networks and systems. Alternatively, breaches can be identified via complaints, unusual or suspicious system behaviour and unavailable functionality of systems or networks. Once an incident or breach has been identified the IRP team needs to be informed, activated and assembled. This is best done via call trees and automatic notification tools. Such tools allow a quick multi-channel notification and also provide status updates like reached, busy, text message delivered etc. Many IRP teams work in virtual environments, i.e. dial into a telephone conference bridge. In some organisations the IRP team meets physically in command centres or control rooms. The activation procedures should be documented, follow a predefined process and be practised regularly to ensure they are effective and operational.

CLASSIFYING THE BREACH

After identifying a cyber incident there are 5 main classifications to further steer the response. The IRP team should classify the incident accordingly to initiate countermeasures, activate other response mechanisms (communications, notifying authorities) and involve the right people in the response. The main classification categories are:

- Attempted Access/Unauthorised Access;

- Denial of Service/Distributed Denial of Service;

- Malicious Code;

- Improper Use; and

- Investigation.

Once the classification has been determined the IRP team needs to deal with the issue and to contain it. There are a variety of response options available. These depend on the type of incident and the individual circumstances. The key is usually to stop or to limit the scope and to ensure critical IT systems are protected and kept available as long as possible. In addition it is essential to understand the current status of systems, networks and data. In order to do so the issue must be isolated and then contained. Some of the most common responses are:

- Disconnect systems from the network and internet;

- Secure firewalls and preserve firewall integrity;

- Disable remote access;

- Restrict traffic for intra/internet;and

- Change access control procedures and passwords.

INCIDENT MANAGEMENT AND CRISIS MANAGEMENT

It may also make sense to create sub-teams depending on the size of the organisation. Many large organisations struggle to get a good command and control structure in place to enable information flows between board/CEO level down to the operational teams dealing with the breach and its containment and vice versa. Smaller organisations have the benefit of size where all relevant parties sit in the same room. A robust Crisis Management organisation is key to ensure communication and coordination of severe incidents flows uninterrupted and includes all relevant departments and topics. Crisis Management is a proven concept originally developed by the military and law enforcement, later successfully adopted by many private sector corporations. In a Crisis Management setup the Incident Management and IRP teams form part of the overall crisis coordination. The most basic determination to differentiate between an incident and a crisis is the impact on the organisation. Many smaller or mid-sized incidents may not pose a threat to the organisation as a whole. A single incident, however, can threaten the very existence of an organisation. It is therefore critical to understand the severity of the incident in order to formulate the right response.

INVESTIGATION, CONTAINMENT AND IMPACTS

Understanding the impacts and investigating the status of systems is the first step to be taken once a response is under way. The IRP team will need to understand what has happened to the systems, networks and data. The impact review should be systematically applied and include:

- Data back-ups including hard drive copies;

- Internal and external storage;

- Network devices;

- System and application logs;

- Real time memories;

- Hand held devices; and

- Data, including private data.

The IRP team should now be in a position to report the type of incident, the impacted systems and associated business processes. This should allow a number of important questions to be answered such as: Who performed the attack? What do the logs tell us about the source of the attack? How can we contain the breach in the short and in the long term? Have we identified quarantined malware and isolated it from the rest of the network? Have we applied all security patches? These questions are supposed to steer the response as well as to allow for a variety of tactics to be applied at the same time. Some call this the active and passive elements of the IRP. The active part is the incident as it happens, i.e. as it is live or active. Here some dramatic action may be required to fight off the attack. The passive component means the analysis of the damage, forensic investigation and following up on root cause and lessons learned.

INTERNAL AND EXTERNAL COMMUNICATION

Effective internal communication is vital to provide an effective response to the incident/breach. First, it is important to be able to reach out to staff either to support the response or to communicate to all staff. The all staff communication is critical to ensure a consistent message across the organisation and to ensure employees do not talk to the press. Best practice is to redirect all inquiries to the press or communications department.

The external communication will then address the wider public including the press. Prepare the preferred channels how you want to inform your clients and the public. This preparation is best documented in a written plan which could be part of your IRP or stand alone. Typically the communications team owns such plans and processes but these can also be embedded into the IRP. It will be crucial to inform the public before the press or social media reports the breach. Any delay in communications may be perceived as you not being in control, not completely aware, indifferent or you have something to hide. Also please consider the authorities, regulators and law enforcement depending on the type of breach.

Any important contacts outside the firm should be documented and maintained in the IRP. These range from key providers, partners, clients, peer groups to authorities and industry bodies.

Any communication should be drafted, reviewed and approved via a pre-defined process. It should also be clear who approves and who owns the internal and external notifications to allow quick communication during the incident.

ERADICATION AND RESTORATION

Following the containment and communication phase the threats leading to the incident must be eradicated and the disrupted processes restored. In order to do so all breach points must be identified and all leavings eradicated. This includes malware, spyware or any other type of software. This can be quite complex and lengthy or require the work of outside experts. Such efforts must also be part of the plan, at least having experts identified so they can be activated at short notice. Should the eradication take longer it is important to consider this in the internal and external communication plans.

At the same time the Business Continuity and Disaster Recovery plans should have been activated. It is critical to consider the root cause and type of breach before such recovery plans are invoked. In some cases it may not be advisable to activate such plans to avoid further damage – for example, failing over an application into disaster recovery mode and therefore copying the malware infecting the application as well. Also, the data backup cycles may need to be paused to avoid copying spyware onto the disks or tapes.

THE IMPORTANCE OF PRACTICE

No plan and no team supposed to implement the plan can be ready without training, practice and exercises. The plan needs to be practised and rehearsed in repeating frequency so that any shortfalls and lessons learned can be used to improve the plan and IRP team. Practising the response also has benefits for the wider response with regard to the people involved. It is always better to let people do something than to tell them in theory what they should do. In many organisations staff felt much more confident after practising their IRPs than those who just had training on it. The frequency and type of exercise strongly depends on the size, culture and industry sector of the organisation. Financial service providers do test annually at least and are required to do so in order to comply with various banking regulations.

IRP LIFECYCLE MAINTENANCE

To wrap up, it is worth bearing in mind that it's not just about good cyber and information security but a robust incident response capability. This includes a planning and testing lifecycle very similar to Business Continuity and Disaster Recovery lifecycles. The plan should be reviewed, updated and tested annually, at least Significant changes should be reflected in the plans right away and not just when the plan review is due. Remember, mishandling a breach can have severe consequences to an organisation's financial, reputational and regulatory standing. Not responding to a breach appropriately could cost a company its life.

2.5 ADDRESSING THE SKILLS SHORTAGE IN CYBER SECURITY

Karla Jobling, BeecherMadden

A LACK OF TALENT IS DRIVING WAGE GROWTH

The number of vacancies in cyber security has increased, year on year, for the past five years. With 50% of vacancies widely expected to remain unfilled by 2020, it is clear there is an issue recruiting the right talent to fill these roles. Employment within the industry remains high; it is rare to speak with a candidate who is not working or immediately available. In 2011, there was still a large number of people suffering the effects of redundancy and companies were able to hire talented individuals quite easily. Since 2012, this has rapidly declined and the market is now totally candidate driven. Candidates will typically have three or four job offers to choose from. There are times when the recruitment process can take two or three months, but there are many candidates who will find they receive job offers within just a couple of weeks of starting their job search. Companies committed to securing the best talent need to have streamlined recruitment processes that are executed quickly.

The key effect of this shortage has been wage growth. Candidates command notable increases in their salary when moving jobs, sometimes up to 25%. In-demand roles pay significantly more now than they did just two years ago. Companies who have not kept up with the salary increases face having their vacancy stay empty for many months and, more likely, will not be able to fill their vacancy at all. For example, it would have been possible in 2012 to recruit a security architect for £70,000. Today, that would be almost impossible, with most architects earning at least £90,000. Many are being paid over £100,000, even up to £120,000 in some cases. With wage growth in the UK hovering at around 2% a year, it is clear that cyber security is outperforming almost all other industries.

The table below illustrates the increases in salaries that those in security have seen. At both entry level and above, wages are higher in 2017 than they were in 2015. While salaries at management level appear to have only increased slightly, this is offset by quicker progression to these levels than in previous years. It can take less time to reach a management position in cyber now than ever before.

Job title	Years of experience	Salary bands 2015	Salary bands 2017
Analyst / Associate	1-3	£20,000-£45,000	£28,000-£40,000
Manager	0-7 years (public sector) 7-12	£25,000-£45,000 £60,000-£75,000	£60,000-£75,000
Senior Manager	7-20	£75,000-£95,000	£75,000-£95,000
Head of	3-7	£45,000-£90,000	£75,000 - £120,000
Director	7-12	£75,000-£150,000	£110,000-£150,000
Global Head / CISO	12-20	£150,000-£300,000	£150,000-£450,000

The most significant salary growth has come for the CISO role. There are now CISO roles paying $1million, and there are a select few global CISOs earning very significant salaries. The change in salaries for this role shows the development of cyber security as an industry. There is significant movement, demand and negotiation when it comes to CISO salaries. Whether this trend will continue, is difficult to predict. Salaries will either rise significantly, based on candidate expectations, or right-size, as companies refuse to keep up with such demands. With the cost of a breach increasing, and increased regulatory interest, many candidates are comparing the cost of their salary to the cost of a potential breach, and feeling under-remunerated.

This increase has largely been due to a recognition of the position of the CISO role. Fewer candidates now hold the job title of CISO if they are not delivering against a typical expectation of that job. In 2014, many CISOs were elevated IT Security Managers, and that has changed. In comparison to 2014 (table below), CISOs are paid at a much higher salary, with very few now earning less than £100,000. The majority of CISOs, are paid between £120,000 and £149,000. Those earning over £200,000 are likely to be operating in a global role and are reporting to the board, or one level below.

Another factor fueling this increase is that CISO roles have also risen in number. BeecherMadden have had a 32% increase in roles this year and many organisations now have a growing security function. Those candidates who have experience leading a security function, operating at board level and communicating the business challenges, can expect to find themselves in demand.

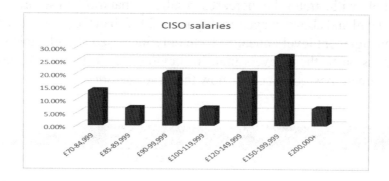

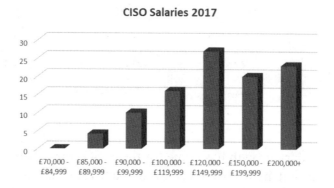

HOW TO FIND CANDIDATES

With a lack of available talent, finding candidates can be difficult. Job adverts have to compete with many others and often can not communicate the real reasons why someone should be interested in that job. Progression and work life balance are listed as the most important reasons for changing job. 84% of candidates considering a move said progression was important to them. Communicating this on a job advert, however, is hard. Using a recruitment agency who knows the market makes this part of the process somewhat easier.

What is important is considering pools of talent that are engaged and easier to attract. This may mean offering training, or re-skilling people. There are a number of apprenticeships and courses now available to young people looking to begin a career in cyber security. These are important for building a future workforce, but will take time to produce results. A much overlooked group are those who are returning to work, or changing careers. Companies that take time to attract these people, will find they have loyal and committed employees, who are engaged with the company they work for.

Many candidates want to enter the cyber security industry. Perhaps they have heard about wage growth or the amount of opportunities. Often, they are interested in the subject and excited about the challenges they will face. Companies who are able to offer training should consider candidates with experience in the following roles, as they often make excellent security professionals and have a number of transferable skills.

- Risk management.

- Project management.

- Compliance.

- Physical security.

HOW TO ATTRACT PEOPLE

There are some key components to devising a successful recruitment strategy.

- Keep the process quick.

- Make the process engaging.

- Be clear on your requirements.

- Only insist on technical tests if it is truly necessary.

- Offer the right salary.

Keep the process quick

All too often, companies take weeks just to review a CV and several more weeks to conduct a first interview. This is often the case for very large organisations, recruiting a high number of candidates at any one time. Candidates may stay engaged in this process because they are keen to work for a large, successful company. However, this is one area where smaller companies can seize the advantage. Taking too long over a recruitment process adds risk, as good candidates will quickly receive jobs offers elsewhere. They also perceive the length of the process as an indicator that the company is not interested in them, and they will lose interest themselves. Companies that are truly committed to hiring the best talent should take the following steps to make sure they move their recruitment process at a reasonable pace.

- Schedule time each week to review CVs. Daily is better, but if a candidate can be told they should expect feedback on a Friday, after the weekly review, they will be more comfortable waiting.

- Schedule time for interviews each week and keep this time free for the coming months. If candidates can be made aware of potential interview times, this will also speed the process up.

- Provide feedback to all candidates, successful or not. Unsuccessful candidates may become clients in the future and they will certainly tell others if your process was not up to scratch.

Make the process engaging

Remember that candidates will have multiple opportunities on offer. It is important that the candidate fully understands the role, the culture and working environment. They need to feel an affinity with your company if you are to ensure they accept your job offer above that of your competitors. Equally, you want to ensure that a candidate who is not a good cultural fit has concluded that before accepting. You do not want to hire someone who will start, only to resign a few months later. There are several things you can do to make the process engaging.

- Give them plenty of time to ask you questions. If you are running an assessment day, schedule time for this. Make sure they feel that you want to answer their questions; don't treat this as a chore.

- Show them the offices and introduce them to others in the team.

- Talk to them about projects they will be working on. If the role is client facing, talk to them about current assignments to make this real, rather than conceptual.

- Talk to them about the growth plans of the company and the long-term goals. Even consider presenting to them; this is a two-way process.

Be clear on your requirements

There are many instances when companies write job descriptions which are vague or unachievable. This is to be expected, as companies may be recruiting for a cyber role for the first time. They may not realise the time requirements of achieving a CISSP or have fully decided what they require from a CISO. By not being totally clear, you are setting yourself up for failure. You will find it harder to recruit the right person but worse, you may recruit the wrong person. The risk of having the wrong person in the job, where neither of you achieve your goals, loses both parties time and money.

- Write a job description which is accurate and truly reflects the requirements of the role. If a qualification is not essential, do not make this a requirement.

- Include deliverables where possible. Put onto paper what you would like a candidate to achieve in their first year. This removes any ambiguity.

- Take advice from consultancies or other companies if this is your first time recruiting for a cyber role. Doing this research upfront will de-risk your recruitment process and improve candidate retention.

Only insist on technical tests if truly necessary

Many roles require a technical test. If you are recruiting a penetration tester, you will want them to demonstrate they can do all the things that they say and are not relying on external tools to do this. Conducting a test can also show you what level they are, benchmarking where they sit within your team. However, there has been an increase in insisting on tests for roles where this is not necessary, slowing the process down and putting candidates off continuing with the interview process.

- Make the test easy to access and complete. Having them undertake this in your office is preferable.

- Provide feedback on the test. You may be able to offer practical advice for their growth, which they will appreciate.

Offer the right salary

This does not have to be the highest salary. If you have shown a candidate good reasons for why they should want to work for you, they may well accept an offer that is lower than another company's. Do ensure that you are making an offer at a level the candidate will accept. Making a low offer makes them feel undervalued and will put them off. While they may then accept if you raise your offer, this will leave them questioning why you could not have offered this salary in the first place.

- Know their current salary and package. Consider all elements of their package including any overtime, bonuses and pension contributions.

- Know the salary they would like to achieve. This includes knowing the salary that makes them jump for joy, and the salary that is the minimum they would accept.

- Provide full details of the total package. If the offer is made of multiple parts, have the full details of this available at the time you present the offer to the candidate. For example, know the exact pension contributions available, know when bonus is paid and how this is achieved, as well as what this has paid out in the past two years.

HOW TO RETAIN YOUR EMPLOYEES

A key trend in the past two years has been to view how companies retain their staff. Between 2013 and 2015, it was common to see candidates change job every year, sometimes less. Candidates were being headhunted daily and offered huge salary increases to change role. They were also being given more responsibility and quickly climbing the corporate ladder. It was not surprising that they were moving jobs so often. Whereas in other industries this would have negatively affected their chances of obtaining a new role, the demand in cyber security was so high, that companies were pleased to have found a suitable employee. The risk that they would soon leave was overlooked or considered to be worth taking.

Since 2015, this trend has decreased. Companies are working harder on retaining their people by showing them career progression and in some cases, changing their requirements to allow candidates to progress in different ways. Consulting firms typically require employees to sell if they wish to reach a senior level. Many firms have changed this requirement, offering progression to those with technical skills who will not sell as part of their role. As security teams have got bigger, there are now more opportunities for an employee to progress, without having to look elsewhere. Between 2016 and 2017, the amount of candidates expecting to receive an internal promotion jumped from 12% to 45%. This is the clearest indicator that companies are working on retaining their talent.

There is also an element of fatigue playing a part in the candidate's psyche. Where individuals are approached daily about new opportunities, these approaches now mean very little. Candidates typically receive a LinkedIn message, broadly similar to all the others, and these are often ignored. They do not look at job adverts as if they were to decide they wanted a new job, they would just have to respond to one of these many messages. This fatigue has served companies well for retention.

By moving jobs often, and with multiple opportunities for networking available, candidates have a good idea of what is happening in the market. They know that the grass is not always greener, and that opportunities elsewhere may be largely the same as those in their current company. Companies that have taken retention seriously have done a good job of communicating this to their current employees. They update them regularly on the successes of the organisation, communicate their growth plans and talk to them about their personal goals. By committing time to retaining their people, they reduce the time they have to spend recruiting and training new ones.

CONCLUSION

There are many factors driving growth in cyber security at the moment. There are a number of steps companies can take to put themselves ahead of the competition, to attract, recruit and retain the best staff. There is, undeniably, a skills shortage in the industry at the moment. Much may change this. AI and an improvement in big data tools may remove some of the roles currently being recruited. Salary growth may reach a level at which a cyber security function is unaffordable, forcing companies to outsource or put a halt on this trend. An increase in the number of candidates available, as more people graduate or change career, may also have an impact. Until these changes happen, companies need to take an honest look at their recruitment process and make necessary changes, to respond to the unique challenges of recruiting in this market.

All data has been taken from BeecherMadden's annual salary surveys.

Part Three

General Data Protection Regulation

3.1 GDPR – A VIEW FROM THE FRONT LINE

Chris Greenslade & John Clelland, Proteus-Cyber Ltd

Surely not another GDPR article? Well, yes! And there will be more to come – this subject is only just getting started. Study after study show how unaware and ill prepared organisations are for the impending GDPR (General Data Protection Regulation), which comes into force on 25th May 2018 and applies to most companies worldwide who hold any personal data on an EU national.

This article gives a personal perspective from a company on the front line of the GDPR, a company that identified early the issues the GDPR would raise and developed a GDPR-specific software tool which was first to market and is still generally considered the most comprehensive GDPR software tool in the market place. We have met with organisations which have the GDPR under control, multinationals which claim they have everything sorted but very clearly haven't, with companies who know they have lost their way and with companies who are hoping to "do GDPR" with no effort at all. We share some observations, identify some frequent pitfalls and provide some tips to help you succeed.

THE NEED FOR THE GDPR

Is it really necessary? Well, in 2016 there were 600 billion records lost through data breaches [ref 1], and these are just the largest ones, highlighting the woefully inadequate protection of data by companies and their IT systems today. So, even though we already have data protection and great security standards such as ISO27001 and PCI, clearly something isn't working. Companies that have certification for these standards have routinely been breached and therefore demonstrated they have not effectively implemented those controls.

The original Data Protection Act was introduced before we had social media or digital business, and at a time when hacking was a computer geek's hobby rather than a cyber criminal's occupation. The term "identity theft" didn't exist and we didn't live our lives online. The first smartphone was still 10 years away! The GDPR updates Data Protection wholesale and looks to address the shortcomings highlighted by the increasingly frequent news stories about breaches; it goes well beyond data protection controls and adds real bite to the data protection bark with fines of up to 4% of global revenue, or £17m if higher.

In layman's terms, the GDPR has taken ownership of data away from the corporate and returned it to the individual. So now you have the right to know what data they hold about you, to have it corrected or transferred to another supplier or to be forgotten (i.e. deleted). Your personal data now also has a value and must be looked after properly – if lost the organisation responsible faces significant financial penalties as well as exposure and you may be entitled to compensation. Covering up data breaches will no longer be tolerated. We heard a Data Protection lawyer describe this as the biggest legislative change in his lifetime. The GDPR is fast approaching – it will be here in just a few months, there is no opt out (unless you have one of the few exemptions) and Brexit will make no difference. The GDPR has to be taken seriously and therefore requires a different approach.

GETTING READY FOR THE GDPR

Having had upwards of 100 conversations with companies at differing stages of readiness for the GDPR we have some anecdotal observations to share on the state of readiness:

1. Most companies will not be GDPR ready by May 25th 2018 [ref 2]. Despite starting well some have lost their way, some as a result of scope creep and many are drowning under Excel spreadsheets, whilst far too many haven't yet started doing anything [ref 3]. We have seen many organisations who have started their data mapping process without adequate thought as to what they will do with the data they collect and how it will help them meet the requirements of the GDPR (e.g. the reporting requirements or handling Subject Access Requests within the prescribed timescales). Before you start data mapping (or anything else) work out how you will demonstrate compliance and work backwards. Engage GDPR lawyers/consultants and use a tool to help guide you through the process. Know where you're going. Our approach is to survey the business owners with just nine questions (we've seen organisations grind to a halt because their survey participants aren't returning their 150 question questionnaires!) to determine what personal data is being collected, for what purpose and how it is categorised. This is then followed up with a technical survey to IT to understand where that data is, how it is secured, with whom it is shared, etc. All this combines to form the data register from which we can produce the article 30 reports. Add in risk assessment, a risk register, project planning, consent management, Subject

Access Request management, breach notification reporting etc., and the story comes together. The Information Commissioner's Office has made it clear that companies that can demonstrate progress against implementation of the GDPR will have this taken in to account in determining the level of fine applicable. Those who have made the least effort or who have repeatedly been breached can expect the harshest treatment.

2. The GDPR isn't an IT task. At its heart is risk (the word is mentioned some 75 times in the regulation) and the GDPR requires a more joined up approach than has conventionally been required for compliance with a standard. Legal and IT need to work with the business functions to address the compliance issues and understand what the risk exposure is and also what risk appetite exists and what level is acceptable to the business. Big questions may be raised by the GDPR; for example, what risk does acquisition of a new company bring or how do we launch a new offering if we don't have the necessary user consent? Only by understanding the risks and mitigations as part of the equation, can proper decision making take place.

3. Specialist help is a must. This follows on from the previous points, but here the point is more about proportionality than direction. Technically the GDPR applies to the great and small alike. Clearly a £1m turnover SME doesn't have the same resource to commit to the GDPR as a £100bn turnover multinational. They want GDPR advice that is specific to their circumstances and is proportional. Chances are they will not spend much more than a token £1-2k addressing the GDPR, so it's important that the money counts. A gap analysis identifying the biggest risks and fixing these (maybe by moving where the data is hosted or encrypting discs) will offer best value for money by targeting spend. Small companies want help from organisations or tools that help them answer their specific questions rather than offer general GDPR advice. There is huge potential for outsourced DPO services by sector (charitable sector, digital marketing, recruitment companies, to name just a few) which have common issues and would pay someone to take the problem away.

4. GDPR specialist advice or software tool? So the anxiety of the GDPR is giving you chest pains. You rush to hospital and are offered a choice: to see a doctor with no technology, or to be offered an angiogram and the best equipment but no doctor? Of course you need both! Your GDPR lawyers/advisors will help you understand the implications of the GDPR for your business whilst the software will guide you through the process efficiently and make the task of handling the resultant data manageable. A question that often amuses us is whether our software is scalable or not. Whilst it is a fair question (and yes, of course it is scalable), it

is often asked by companies sinking under hundreds of Excel spreadsheets. We all love our spreadsheets and they are well suited to certain tasks. However, in our opinion, they are one of the least scalable technologies out there and should not be used to undertake process impact assessments or data privacy impact assessments unless the organisation is very small. We have been asked to help numerous large corporates to digest their spreadsheets and build a data registry from which they can report. Whilst we can do this using our import tools, a better approach would be to use online surveys rather than spreadsheets. So GDPR lawyers/advisors apply the regulations to the business, whilst software enables the compliance process both this year and the year after. That's important because the GDPR is here to stay and its obligations are ongoing. The ability to report and manage compliance remains and a specialised GDPR software tool will be required if you want to maintain compliance without rerunning the consultancy exercise. Rather, use the experts to focus on the bigger questions, such as the impact of the GDPR on impending changes and upcoming opportunities within the business. Finally, GDPR lawyers/ consultants bring independence whereas software brings consistency. Both play important parts in a good GDPR implementation.

5. We've heard our country is ahead – true? Our sample really isn't big enough to say definitively, but we have had most contact from Germany, Italy and the UK with interest from Denmark, France, Holland, Greece, Portugal and Spain. What is more interesting is which companies consider themselves well placed and which don't and the reasons for such confidence. There is wide variation and confidence doesn't always equate with readiness based on what we have seen! We believe that there is still sufficient time to get ready provided you have a clear process for assessing your business and for demonstrating compliance.Obviously you may find areas that require remedial work and the time that takes to address will be determined by the issue and your ability to fix it. So it's all about your readiness rather than your country's readiness. Talk about certain countries' supervising authorities being more lenient than others is a distraction in our opinion, as one of the aims of the GDPR is to apply consistency across member states.

6. The GDPR should be seen as an opportunity. It's a real opportunity to strengthen your data-handling and therefore resilience to data breach. Whilst the fines associated with the GDPR are likely to galvanise activity, the real prize is realised in the reduced likelihood of a data breach. Reputational damage is still generally the biggest cost following a breach. Compliance with the GDPR serves to improve business resilience and increase consumer confidence. Private consumer data can no longer be handled without care. Care is a core part of customer satisfaction and confidence. Whilst today consumers may have resigned themselves to data losses, they will not be so accepting in the future. The GDPR is a catalyst for

improvement and should be grasped positively and welcomed by businesses, especially B2C, where confidence matters.

7. Is there a better way? We've said enough earlier about what isn't working. But let's briefly consider one aspect of why it isn't working. IT departments tend to deploy their Digital Risk Management in silos. This disjointed implementation, together with the ever-increasing complexity of systems and means by which they may be accessed, leads to breaches. The GDPR must be implemented in a unified way in order to operate effectively. Only when the various business functions work together can risk truly be addressed, and risk is at the heart of the GDPR.

8. What matters most under GDPR? After 'not getting breached' we would say it is the ability to *demonstrate* compliance against the regulation. The General Counsel of a Fortune 100 organisation that has our Proteus®GDPReady™ software installed said that if he was audited then it would be the first few minutes that would count; if he could show that he was in control and could demonstrate this using the software right up front, then he would have an easy ride; if not, it would be tough going thereafter. So whilst the data mapping needs to be done in order for reporting to be possible, we think the value lies in the reporting. We go further and link the business process/data mapping, lawful basis for processing, IT data handling, third party processor audits, consent rules in T&Cs and subject access requests so that they are coordinated. This makes responding to a breach request within a reasonable time possible. Good preparation, combined with fast, comprehensive reporting, earns credibility with the authorities. If you can demonstrate that you are in control, you most likely are in control, and that is good for business.

10 TOP TIPS

These are not the ICO's 12 steps or particularly all-encompassing, but rather tips based on what we have learned on the journey so far:

1. Don't treat the GDPR as just another standard – it's much more than that and will likely take longer to address.

2. GDPR should be on the corporate risk register and owned by the board. Involve IT but don't assign the task to them. Appoint a board sponsor, if not the CEO.

3. Appoint a DPO as soon as possible. Your DPO should report into the board independently.

4. Avoid scope creep – the GDPR is a big enough task. For now, just do what is necessary to comply with the GDPR (e.g. PIA/DPIAs, data registry, article 30 reports, breach notification reports etc). You can always do more later on.

5. Before you start, consider what you really want to achieve: ability to demonstrate compliance against the GDPR, ability to report (article 30 reports), Subject Access Requests handling, consent management, breach notifications, data register, etc. Then consider the best way to get the data you need to deliver these.

6. Consider how you will store and access the data you collect. Avoid Excel unless you are relatively small. But if you must use it, work out how you will bring all those spreadsheets together into a single data register. Who can see it? What can they see (e.g. only data belonging to a particular department, business unit, division, country, company or group)?

7. Use GDPR consultants/lawyers to apply GDPR to your industry and to work through some of the very difficult business questions the GDPR raises (such as agility v compliance or M&A implications).

8. Minimise reliance on 'consent' if possible as it can be withdrawn; preferably find another lawful basis for processing. Review consents and T&Cs accordingly.

9. Once you think you are compliant, consider how you will remain compliant. How will you verify the information collected next year and the year after (spreadsheets are looking out of place again).

10. If you haven't yet started, start now. If you are behind, just keep going. May 25th isn't the end date, it's the start date. The GDPR is here to stay, so avoidance is not an option. Better to get ahead of the curve and view it as competitive advantage.

3.2 GENERAL DATA PROTECTION REGULATION (GDPR) – INTRODUCING THE UK REGIME

Dan Hyde, Penningtons Manches LLP

It is hard to imagine that anyone involved in running a business has not now heard of the General Data Protection Regulation (GDPR) yet this regulation, which was conceived and born in the European Union, was largely ignored until the clock started ticking and it began to dawn that non-compliance was not an option and that businesses that were caught out by this regulation would need to adapt or face crippling fines.

The first question that needs answering is whether the GDPR applies to your business. It should be noted that the GDPR has extra-territorial effect so that it applies to all businesses offering goods or services in the European Union or monitoring individuals in the European Union. It applies whether or not the business has any branch or office in the EU or indeed any server. In short, the GDPR will apply to most if not all businesses that have an EU customer base. This is because it focuses on the protection of the European individual's data, wherever that data may be.

The GDPR is to be in force in all European Union member states on 25 May 2018. The United Kingdom will still be a member state on that date and the GDPR will consequently become UK law on that date. There are a number of derogations which are specific options that the GDPR allows member states to decide upon. At around the same time as the GDPR becomes UK law, the new UK Data Protection Bill will commence and that will largely reflect the GDPR but will introduce some UK specific variations that are permitted. An example of this is that the GDPR allows a member state to decide whether a child is defined as 16 or under but the UK has decided to opt for 13 so that a 13 year old will be able to consent whereas a younger child will need parental consent.

Once you have decided whether the GDPR will apply to your business you next need to understand the most important concepts in GDPR and data protection. The first of these is *'data processing'*. Any operation performed on personal data such as collection, recording, organising, structuring, storage, adaptation, retrieval, consultation, use, disclosure by transmission, making available or transferring, disseminating or deleting will constitute data processing. Virtually any action in relation to personal data will constitute data processing; a *'data subject'* is the person the data is about, for example a customer or patient is a data subject when their personal data is processed for a purpose of the business. We will look at some of the legitimate purposes later in this chapter. Of particular importance is the *'data controller'*; this is the person or entity (whether public or private) that collects and processes the personal data. The controller determines the purposes and means of processing personal data and has extensive obligations under the GDPR. Finally, *'personal data'* means exactly that, data which relates to any identifiable person who can be directly or indirectly identified by reference to an identifier. This definition is wide as even personal data that has been pseudonymised or anonymised can fall within the scope of the GDPR but this will depend upon how difficult or possible it is to identify the particular individual despite the use of the pseudonym or anonymous title. In summary, the GDPR will apply to personal information (widely defined) and will govern the actions of the controllers and processors of that personal information (very widely defined).

The GDPR places legal obligations on both controllers and processors and general principles that run through GDPR must be applied. The general principles are:

- Lawful fairness and transparency – data has to be processed in accordance with EU and member state laws and data controllers have to be transparent with customers regarding what happens to their personal data. Handling personal information in a legitimate way and ensuring transparency as to how that personal data is handled is at the heart of the GDPR.

- Purpose limitation – the data has to be collected for a specific explicit and legitimate purpose. It cannot be used for other purposes beyond that specific explicit legitimate purpose. What is legitimate will be looked at later in this chapter.

- Data minimisation – you should only request information that is required and relevant for the purpose for which the data is being collected. This is the *de minimis* rule so that the data controller should only request the minimum amount of information that is needed for the specific explicit legitimate purpose.

- Accuracy – data controllers must ensure that their data is accurate. If not, it should be rectified. The data must be kept up to date and every reasonable step should be taken to ensure that it is accurate with regard to the purpose for which it is being processed and where inaccuracies are discovered data should be erased or rectified without delay.

- Limited storage – data should only be stored for a limited period and except for archiving and scientific research purposes it should not be stored beyond the life of the specific explicit and legitimate purpose.

- Integrity and confidentiality – data has to be processed in a way that minimises the risk to its confidentiality and integrity. This should include protection against unlawful or unauthorised processing or accidental damage or loss.

- Accountability – the data controller must be seen to be accountable. This means you must be in a position to prove that the general principles are being applied and that the burden of proof is on the data controller to show this is the case.

In order to process personal information you must identify a legitimate reason for doing so otherwise the processing will not be lawful under the GDPR. The legitimate reason that is relied upon must be documented.

There must then be a legitimate purpose (lawful basis) for processing personal data and these are as follows:

1. That you have the consent of the data subject. This is dealt with in detail later but it will be essential to document that the consent has been given.

2. That processing is necessary for the performance of a contract with a data subject or to take steps to enter into a contract. This then is the contractual purpose.

3. That processing is required to comply with a legal obligation that the data controller must meet.

4. That processing is necessary to protect the vital interests of the data subject or another person.

5. That the processing is necessary for the performance of a task in the exercise of official authority vested in the controller or something that is in the public interest.

6. That the processing is necessary for the legitimate interest of the controller or a third party. This will include the commercial interests of the controller as

such interests are capable of being a legitimate interest. The test is whether the interest of the controller is overridden by the interests, rights or freedoms of the data subject. A balancing act needs to be performed to ensure that where legitimate business interests are pursued, they are not overtaken by the interests, rights and freedoms of the data subject whose personal information is being used for the purpose.

It is important to select the most appropriate lawful basis for processing; if, for example, the legitimate purpose relied upon is the consent of the data subject there will be problems if in due course the data subject withdraws their consent. With this in mind it is advisable to chose and document, where possible, another legitimate interest as that avoids the situation where the consent is withdrawn or cannot be demonstrated, and the controller is left holding information which has no lawful basis.

There are, however, special categories of data where explicit consent of the data subject will be required. Personal data that is categorised as special category personal data will require a higher hurdle in order to justify that its processing is legitimate. Special category personal data is any data that reveals racial or ethnic origin, political opinion, religious or philosophical beliefs, trade union membership or genetic data, biometric data for the purpose of identifying a person or data concerning health or data concerning a person's sex life or sexual orientation. Should you seek to process this sort of data, then under the GDPR this is prohibited unless the data subject has given explicit consent to its processing for one or more specified purposes. There are limited exceptions to this, for example where the processing is necessary to protect the vital interests of the data subject or another person, where the data subject is physically or legally incapable of giving consent or where the processing relates to personal data which has manifestly been made public by the data subject and is thus in the public domain already but exceptions will be of limited application. There is a further exception for processing where it is necessary for the purposes of preventative or occupational medicine or management of health or social care systems and services pursuant to a contract with a heath care professional. This exception will only apply to the healthcare and occupational medicine arena; ancillary uses such as health insurance will not fall within it and explicit consent will be required.

To constitute explicit consent there must be unambiguous consent to the use of the special category data. This must be an affirmative action by the data subject with demonstrable proof that explicit unambiguous consent to the use of the data was given. This means an act that has been freely given and is a clear indication of the client's agreement to the processing of their personal data. Where there is a significant difference in power between the data subject and controller, such as between an employee and employer, it will likely be presumed that consent was not freely given. Silent or inactive consent, such as a pre-ticked box, would also not be considered as consent although a box which has been deliberately ticked would suffice as that would indicate active consent so long as there was proper information as to the use the data was to be put to.

The key here is to remember that the burden of proof is with you and that you need to show that the consent given was informed, intelligible and easily accessible. It should be expressed in clear and plain language and be distinguishable from other matters. A signed form that includes a number of other matters would fall foul of this unless the consent to the use of the personal information could be clearly identified and understood. It should also be plain that any customer had been informed before giving consent that they were able to withdraw it and that children (in the UK this is defined as those aged below 13) have parental consent as otherwise their data cannot be lawfully processed.

In order to be transparent and comply with the GDPR, when a data controller collects the personal information from the data subject they have to give, at the time they collect the data, the following information:

1. The identity of the contact person or data controller;

2. The purpose for which the data is being processed;

3. The period for which the data will be stored (this can be an estimate at the outset);

4. If it is intended to transfer the data to another country;

5. If the business wishes to process the customer data for another secondary purpose in addition to the specific explicit purpose that have been given; and

6. Explain the data subject's rights, namely:

    a. That they have the right to be kept informed and to access their own personal data and these are fundamental rights;

    b. That they have a right to data portability so that they can transfer data from one data controller to another;

    c. That they have the right to object to the processing of their data; and

    d. That they have the right to request rectification of their data if it is inaccurate or incomplete;

e. That they have the right to deletion of their data, known as the right to be forgotten. This might apply where a data subject has withdrawn consent and no other lawful basis remains that can justify the storage or processing of their data or that the principles of limited storage and data minimisation support the request for deletion;

f. That they have a right to restrict the processing of their data; and

g. That they also have rights in relation to any automated processing and profiling.

It is important to note these rights; the rights of the individual are at the very core of the GDPR and organisations should strive to ensure they can document their application. In practical terms you will need to implement internal policies that ensure all the key information is documented, which will ensure you record the legitimate lawful basis for processing and where consent is relied upon it is properly recorded. In relation to special category data the record will need to demonstrate explicit consent.

Businesses will be required to designate an independent and appropriately skilled Data Protection Officer (DPO) where the organisation is a public body or where the core activities involve regular and systematic monitoring of personal data on a large scale or the processing of special categories of data or large scale processing of sensitive data. The likelihood is that unless your business crunches significant amounts of personal or sensitive information as its primary activity then it will not be forced to designate a DPO, so if this activity is secondary or ancillary this requirement should not bite. That said, in the light of the burdens of recording and accountability brought by the GDPR, organisations should carefully consider appointing a DPO where funds allow and the role would otherwise eat in to the time of other personnel.

The GDPR is also a game changer in the event of a data breach. There will be mandatory notification of a cyber security breach to the supervisory authority without undue delay and, in any event, no later than 72 hours if there is a risk to individual rights and freedoms. This will nearly always apply unless encryption or other defence mechanisms have kept the data absolutely intact and uncompromised. Where a report is late then a reasoned justification for the delay must be made. This all then goes back to the raison d'etre of the GDPR, the protection of the individual's data rights – a risk in relation to their rights and freedoms must be notified to the Information Commissioners Office (ICO) and, if it is a high risk then the individual also must be notified. There is then a dual test: a mere requires notification to the ICO and a high risk requires additional notification to the individuals whose personal information has been affected. There are very limited exceptions to this such as where encryption or other protection is in place but in such a situation there would not be high risk. The other is where individual notifications would be disproportionate and a public information campaign or other method might better meet the need for information.

Companies with failures in relation to notification of breaches can be fined the greater of 10 million euros or 2% of worldwide annual turnover for the preceding financial year. Other breaches could be double that and the greater of 20 million or 4% of worldwide annual turnover. Those sums are the maximums and we will need to watch how the ICO pitches the level of these fines after 25 May 2018; my guess is that there will be some hefty early punishments to put down a marker and preparing properly should ensure business survival in this tough new compliance landscape.

3.3 USING SCENARIO WORKSHOPS TO PREPARE FOR THE GDPR AND OTHER LEGISLATION

Richard Preece, Oakas Ltd

THE PROBLEM SITUATION

Providing leadership, governance and executive management has never been more challenging. This arises from the continuing trends of increasing complexity, dynamism and uncertainty linked to hyper-connection, encapsulated as the *Digital Age*. This means that a core challenge for company directors and officers is having to make decisions and apply judgement more quickly in an environment that is less understood.

Research suggests that people make good decisions in contexts in which they have experience, good information and prompt feedback. They tend to do less well in contexts in which they are inexperienced and poorly informed, and in which feedback is slow or infrequent. This includes making decisions about the future, based upon trends and known complex changes, which haven't yet materialised.[1] So, the better the understanding of the *Digital Age* environment, the better informed strategy and execution decisions will be. But how to achieve this?

One tried and tested method is to use scenario planning and workshops.[2] Perhaps the most important benefit of this approach is that it can take a seemingly abstract

---

1. There is a large amount of literature in this area, much building upon the work of Professor Daniel Kahneman (Nobel Laureate) and Dr Amos Tversjy who researched the effects of heuristics (rules of thumb) and biases (tendencies) in human judgement.

2. This concept dates back to the Prussian Army in the 1820s. It was subsequently successfully adopted by other militaries and is still used extensively for strategic and tactical planning in all leading militaries. In the 1970s Shell developed scenario planning in the oil and gas industry, which has been adopted more widely across other sectors, to support strategy and operational excellence.

future concept and bring it to life. In particular, it provides a safe environment for multi-disciplinary teams and stakeholders to develop shared understanding of a problem's structure and context. This enables individuals and teams to relate their existing knowledge and skills to new situations and concepts. In doing so they are better able to anticipate issues and risks and apply their problem solving and critical-thinking skills, supported by feedback.

Scenario workshops are just one tool to do this, but are probably the simplest and most cost-effective way to start the process. Initially they can be used to gain shared understanding and buy-in; subsequently they can look at specific issues in greater detail.

STRATEGIC QUESTIONS

In the previous book in this series, in the chapter *Reviewing and Updating Contingency Plans*, we identified the importance of starting with the end in mind. From this, three questions that company directors and officers need to answer and to continue to ask, were identified and explored:

1. *"Business growth and return on investment – do we understand where our value is and what the cyber risk (including opportunity) is to it?"*;

2. *"Could we defend our level of preparation and response in the aftermath of a cyber incident?"*; and

3. *"Has the situation changed?"*

These simple questions are intended to help company directors and officers to direct and provide strategic alignment, leadership and culture, governance and accountability. In turn, this should lead to prioritised and ongoing resourced risk management and the development of capability to act.

Applying these simple questions to current and upcoming legislation is increasingly necessary. This is driven by our increasing individual and collective digital dependency, which is creating new and amplified risks to society, economy, organisations and people. This legislation is taking many forms globally, which in itself raises complexity and compliance costs for many companies. However, the European Union (EU) have produced two recent and far-reaching examples of this trend: the General Data Protection Regulation (GDPR) and the Network Information Security Directive (NISD).

In both cases they are due to be applied from May 2018. There will be some national variations, such as the British Data Protection Bill, which introduces additional criminal sanctions, whilst there is a current Security and Network Information Public Consultation, for Operators of Essential Services (OES).

GDPR and NISD are concerned with specific individual privacy, and societal and economic safety and security respectively. However, in both cases, there is clear potential for reputational, operational, financial and commercial material impact upon companies. Therefore, the fiduciary duties of company directors and officers require them to consider how to best manage the risks.

GDPR: CASE IN POINT

The GDPR states a number of obligations and duties with which companies must comply. GDPR compliance is not achieved through a simple rules and standards framework, which often leads to a simple tick-box culture. Instead it has adopted a principles and contextual risk-based approach, centred upon protecting the rights and privileges of individuals.

For companies and in particular for company directors and officers, who have fiduciary duties to protect and grow long term value, this has become an even more complex, dynamic and uncertain task. Provisions within the GDPR for the competent supervisory authority, i.e. the UK Information Commissioner's Office (ICO), to impose regulatory fines of up to €20m, or up to 4%, of the total worldwide annual turnover of the preceding financial year, whichever is higher in certain circumstances, have led to some significant headline spin![3]

This means understanding Data Protection by Design/Default, which is often referred to as *Privacy by Design*. This is articulated within the GDPR, but is not defined in detail. This is a sensible legislative approach that seeks to make privacy a business issue, by developing and maintaining accountable business practices and to avoid tick-box compliance culture. Ultimately, it seeks to enable businesses to exploit the innovative opportunities of the *Digital Age* and to consider proactively the potential impact of new operating models, products and services. This is also the general approach articulated by the UK's National Cyber Security Centre (NCSC) for cyber security in general.[4]

So corporate directors and officers need to make evidence based decisions and cut through the spin! Judgement should be applied to new and amplified financial, reputational, operational and commercial material impact risks. However, this should be balanced with opportunities to assess new strategies, operating models, goods and services from a different perspective and to potentially increase innovation. Ultimately, the GDPR requires a deeper understanding of privacy risks and the application of demonstrable governance and action to mitigate these risks for both Data Subjects and to protect the business.

---

3. This issue was recently reflected by the UK ICO in her blog: https://iconewsblog.org.uk/2017/08/09/gdpr-sorting-the-fact-from-the-fiction/.

4. The NCSC Secure by Default webpage is a good source for further information: https://www.ncsc.gov.uk/topics/secure-default

The GDPR requires taking appropriate action to proactively protect "*the rights and freedoms*" of Data Subjects and to mitigate any effects of a breach. From this perspective, *risk* is a scenario describing an event and its consequences, estimated in terms of likelihood and severity of impact upon the Data Subject. Data Protection Impact Assessments (DPIAs) are required when there is likely high risk "*to the rights and freedoms of individuals.*" From a GDPR perspective, rights primarily concern the Right to Privacy, but may also involve other fundamental rights such as Freedom of Speech, Freedom of Thought, Freedom of Movement, Prohibition of Discrimination and the Right to Liberty, Conscience and Religion.

Privacy impacts can manifest in different ways. Summarising guidance from the UK ICO, some may be direct 1st order effects, with tangible and quantifiable impacts, e.g. financial loss or losing a job. Other more indirect 1st order effects may have intangible and less quantifiable impacts, e.g. damage to personal relationships and social standing arising from disclosure of confidential or sensitive information. There may also be direct 2nd order effects, where privacy harm may be real even if it is not obvious, e.g. the fear of identity theft that comes from knowing that the security of information could be compromised. Finally, there may be indirect 2nd order effects, when privacy harm may also go beyond the immediate impact on individuals. Harm may arise from the use of personal information which may be imperceptible or inconsequential to individuals, but cumulative and substantial in its impact on society, e.g. it may contribute to a loss of personal autonomy or dignity or exacerbate fears of excessive surveillance.

So, compliance with GDPR requires clearly thinking through and assessing potential scenarios from the perspective of the individual's rights and freedoms. As a company, the potential effects of privacy risks need to be assimilated into the wider strategy for the business, including integrating wider information/cyber security strategy, risk management and the investments and the necessary capability and cultural changes. This is Question 1 above: "*Business growth and return on investment?*" Not being able to demonstrate having been through the process and to have considered the *so-whats* exposes companies and their directors and officers to potentially significant negative impacts. This is Question 2 above: "*Could we defend our level of preparation and response?*"

GDPR: CONDUCTING A SCENARIO WORKSHOP

Scenario workshops can and probably should be conducted at various points in the preparation for the GDPR. But who, when, where and how to conduct scenario workshops for the GDPR? There are two main types of circumstances in which to conduct scenario workshops.

The first type of circumstance is focused upon governance, accountability and strategy. The purpose is to deepen individual and shared understanding of those who are accountable and have key responsibilities for data protection, namely company directors and officers. Good practice such as the UK's Corporate Governance Code 2012, identifies that boards should ensure the competence and capacity of its members. Furthermore, the board's expectations should be stated in policies, and then regularly reviewed and updated as necessary, to ensure that they remain aligned with its changing context. As articulated above, the GDPR and wider cyber security is an example that requires this, due to the potential material impact upon a company.

So as part of any GDPR awareness package, scenario workshops provide an opportunity for company directors and officers to deepen their understanding of the GDPR. By collectively taking this group through the experience of a privacy breach scenario, it enables them to be provided with the *good* information and prompt feedback that was identified previously as the key to good decision-making and to apply their judgement.

By conducting scenario workshops in a structured, facilitated and confidential environment, it enables the achievement of twin objectives. First, making decisions specifically to support *Privacy by Design* and compliance with the GDPR and other legislation. Second, making decisions and providing direction for wider strategy, investments and general (cyber) risk management.

The second type of circumstance is when reviewing current data processing and new projects and programmes and the conduct of DPIAs. The purpose of DPIA is to examine risk to the privacy of Data Subjects. A DPIA does not require a scenario workshop, but it is potentially an efficient and effective method to assess both privacy and wider business risk. Conducting a scenario workshop as part of a DPIA can help to ensure that potential problems are identified at an early stage. Often addressing these earlier will be simpler, less costly and enable effective balance of investment and strategy decisions.

Depending upon how strategic a particular programme or project is, this type of scenario workshop is unlikely to require participation from company directors and officers as a matter of routine. However, there should be processes and structures in place to enable oversight of the outputs. But if as part of the wider DPIA process a *"high-risk to the rights and freedoms"* of Data Subjects is identified, then participation of key individuals and their teams is highly recommended. This is Question 3 above: *"Has the situation changed?"* This could include Data Protection Officers (DPO), or equivalents,[5] General Counsel, Chief Information Officers (CIOs), Chief Information Security Officers (CISOs) and other key individuals.

Scenario workshops in both types of circumstances should involve multiple-views and expertise. In the case of DPIAs, the involvement of some Data Subjects and

---

5. GDPR requires certain organisations to have a DPO, which is a protected position; a DPO is not accountable for Data Protection, the Board is. However, good practice is to have a privacy advocate and someone who can help bring about change; these can be internal or externally appointed to a company.

other external stakeholders may be appropriate and is consistent with good practice. However, the outputs and outcomes from scenario workshops in either circumstance should be to enable company directors and officers to join the dots between the requirements of GDPR and Privacy by Design and their wider fiduciary duties.

Where a scenario workshop is conducted is a matter of choice. However, often it can form an important part of an away-day, whether specifically considering privacy and the GDPR or as part of general strategy and governance.

Again, how to conduct a scenario workshop is a matter of choice. However, experience suggests that it should have a sponsor, who articulates the business aim and purpose of the workshop to all at the beginning, so setting the scene. Depending upon the familiarity of the participants with the subject, it may be appropriate to provide an information or awareness briefing and discussion as part of establishing shared understanding. Pre-reading is helpful; however, a good briefing and facilitation to provide the structure and context of the problem should be sufficient to enable company directors and officers to apply their judgement to the issues.

Once this level baseline has been achieved a simple contextual risk-based scenario can be used to stimulate discussion and problem-solving. This requires an element of analysis and preparation in advance. A main events list, captured on slides and using injections on slides and other media are all that is required for a basic scenario workshop. For strategic scenario workshops, the focus should generally not be on the technicalities, but upon the impact on the Data Subjects and how the incident would be handled by the company and likely business impacts. From this a number of observations, lessons and recommendations for further action can be identified through analysis.

This then can form the basis for further action or risk treatment. It also can enable the board to explicitly document expectations of themselves and of those to whom they delegate data protection and wider cyber security responsibilities. Throughout this process, GDPR and good governance practice generally require that this is documented and held for record. This becomes particularly important in the event of any investigation following a data breach, in which the relevant supervising authority will look for evidence of governance activities and DPIAs having been carried out. Effectively no documentation means no evidence, which means potentially more severe administrative fines and other actions.

In summary, scenario workshops are a proven tool that can be used by company directors, officers and those that support them. They can be used to prepare for compliance with the GDPR by demonstrating an aspect of *Privacy by Design*. Scenario workshops are potentially highly efficient in terms of cost and time, and effective in developing understanding and supporting decision-making.

3.4 GDPR– COMPARATIVE INTERNATIONAL REGIMES

Dan Hyde, Penningtons Manches

The approach to the protection of data and cybersecurity are some one of the most significant issues facing governments, organisations and individuals. Such has been the understandable fanfare around the pending implementation (25 May 2018) of the General Data Protection Regulations (GDPR) in all EU Member States, that many are acutely aware and fearful of the new regulatory landscape and the fines that will follow non-compliance. What far fewer appreciate is that it has wider cultural ramifications. The introduction of uniform data regulation across Europe has highlighted the different approach to data and cyber security regulation elsewhere; we may be witnessing the start of a philosophical divergence in the treatment of information protection across the globe. This chapter examines some of the international comparative regimes that are at play when one ventures beyond the land of the GDPR and the issues that a business may face when conducting global business.

In terms of international personal data transfers the GDPR allows transfers to another country or international entity within the European Union and this should be straightforward as the transfer is essentially from one GDPR regulated state to another. International transfers to a third country or entity outside the EU are also permitted but the regulatory regime of that recipient country must be deemed to provide an "adequate" level of data protection. An organic list of adequate regimes will develop and add to or deduct from those countries presently considered adequate. To be adequate the regime has to provide an equivalent level of data protection ("equivalence") so the bar is set high. Where the regime isn't considered adequate transfers will still be allowed subject to the use of standard contractual clauses or binding corporate rules. There is also a scheme that permits transfers where there are certifications and binding enforceable commitments on the part of the data controller or processor which invoke sufficient safeguards. Whilst a small number of countries may reach the dizzy heights of equivalence there are, in truth, no international regimes that precisely mirror the philosophy or application of the GDPR.

The GDPR is the first attempt at a unified law to govern the collection, control and processing of personal data. But law is rarely without politics, and politics can be geographically sensitive. Significantly, the GDPR emphasises the rights and freedoms of the individual citizen and the sanctity of an individual's personal data. This runs root and branch through the GDPR; from the need to show an individual has given active and demonstrable consent through to the embedded rights of the data subject (individual) to ensure that organisations only keep data for the purposes specified in the GDPR and that a data subject has a 'right to be forgotten.' This development ought to ensure that there is a sea change in the way that entities who are subject to European jurisdiction treat personal data. They become mere custodians of someone else's valuable property (the individual's data) and they are required to deal with that personal data in a way that is consistent with handling someone else's item of significant value. There are individual rights of redress built into the GDPR and evidence will be required to show that dealings in personal data have been conducted appropriately. In Europe then, the rights of the individual in relation to their data have been recognised as paramount. The UK will similarly adhere to this edict (there is no doubt as to that) and one might have hoped for global uniformity on the regulation and philosophical treatment of information. Or perhaps not. Significant cybersecurity legislative initiatives have occurred in China, Russia and the United States. The result is a divergence in philosophy and a rejection of the European model of individual data protection values. These major comparative regimes differ in material respects.

In the cases of China and Russia the role of the State in data protection and management has been placed at the epicentre of regulation. Data sovereignty or data of the state are the guiding and dominant policies at play. The State, not the individual, is paramount.

THE RUSSIAN REGIME

In Russia, on 1 September 2015, the Russian Federation passed a law which required personal data relating to Russian citizens to be stored on servers physically located within the country. For Russia, such information belonged to Russia and it would remain within its national borders. Russian personal data had to remain Russian and within Russia.

Companies including Viber and Ebay complied, and moved relevant personal data to Russian servers. Google reportedly also complied. Facebook, Twitter and LinkedIn, decided not to comply with the new requirements. Roskomnadzor, the Russian regulator, sued LinkedIn for non-compliance, and won its case twice, first in a lower court in August and then again, on 10 November 2016, in a Moscow city court. At this point access was blocked.

Roskomnadzor made it clear compliance would require moving Russian users' data onto Russian soil and by amending its user agreement that states that the company collects not only personal data of its users but also personal metadata (IP addresses and cookie files) of its website's visitors. In Russia, then, Nation State regulation and data sovereignty trump individual data rights. The GDPR, its notions and philosophy of individual freedoms and rights, has no place in Russia.

THE CHINESE REGIME

China's new Cyber Security Law commenced on 1 June 2017. It should be noted that prior to 1 June 2017, any European model of personal data protection law had not been recognisable in China. Indeed, China had not previously passed any meaningful comprehensive data protection legislation that regulated the collection, control and processing of personal information. On 1 June that changed; but whilst China's Cyber Security Law does give a nod to protection of an individual's rights, it has State interest and sovereignty at its heart.

The new Chinese Cyber Security Law impacts on what it terms 'network operators' who, when handling personal information, must abide by regulations that chime with the GDPR general principles namely (in broad terms) that:

- The collection and use of personal information must be lawful, proper and necessary;

- The purpose, method, and scope of collection and the use is transparent and consensual;

- They do not disclose, alter, or destroy personal data without appropriate consent;

- They report data breaches and effect remedial steps; and

- They deal with requests for deletion (akin to the right to be forgotten) or correction where information is inaccurate.

But this nod to the protection of the individual is secondary to the interests and sovereignty of the State. The definition of "network operators" in the Cyber Security Law is so widely drawn that it would cover even the domestic user with nothing more than a single computer (or indeed a device such as a phone) with access to a printer. In short, almost everyone is caught and those deemed "critical information infrastructure operators" ('CIIOs') are forced to physically store within China (within its geographical borders) any personal information and important data which was produced within China. In short this Chinese data must be physically kept on servers within China, thus chiming with the law in Russia. Chinese personal data is Chinese and must remain in China.

The State may also conduct what are termed "security risk assessments" to trawl through all the data of an organisation or individual. The new Cyber Security Law allows extensive state intrusion and is aimed at keeping 'critical' Chinese data in China. This is state data sovereignty at its highest. The definition of CIIOs is so broad and malleable as to ensure China can exert influence wherever it sees fit and it applies to non-Chinese operators as well as those in China because no distinction is made between internal or external networks. In practice the State will strive to ensure personal information it regards as important remains on servers within China and any attempt to transfer it will then be subject to the "genuine business need test" following an intrusive state assessment.

THE US REGIME

In the US there is no single uniform analogous regulation but rather a myriad of state regulations and federal rules. The US does give a nod to protecting the individual's privacy, but the right of an individual in relation to their data could be said to have been diminished by the repeal of regulations requiring internet service providers to do more to protect customers' privacy than websites like Google or Facebook.

This initiative, founded during the currency of the Obama Administration, had sought to restrict the ability of internet providers to use sensitive information such as location, financial information, information in relation to health and web browsing history for advertising and marketing purposes. The previous rules made it unlawful to use such information without obtaining appropriate consent. The decision of the Senate to vote down these provisions was based on the assertion that it would lead to a different set of regulations for internet providers and websites. The sale of personal information collected by retailers is huge business in the US. The focus is on the corporate rather than the individual and in the US the corporate is sacrosanct.

The really significant issue is how businesses can, and if it is even possible to, mesh these different approaches.

Whilst in the case of Russia and China, the centre of data protection and management vests in the State, that is not the case in Europe and seemingly, the United States. In Europe the individual is paramount. In the United States, corporations appear to have scored a major victory. So where does that leave the possibility of a consistent approach to data protection and management across the world? – In tatters. A global entity doing business in each of the jurisdictions discussed above will be faced with regimes and policies which are at odds with each other. How will, for example, an entity free to sell personal data in the US deal with the need to obtain active and demonstrable consent to such a course of action in Europe? The requirement in Russia or China to ensure that data is subjected to scrutiny by the State will impact on the rights of the subject if they are European. The GDPR envisages only allowing data transfers to jurisdictions that have 'adequate' measures to ensure consistency and equivalence of approach. The ability to sell personal data for advertising purposes does not sit well with the cornerstone of the sanctity of an individual's personal data.

Another problem area will be where an organisation (or individual) in Europe has dealings in Russia and has to be subject to state scrutiny of its personal data. Will the relevant supervisory authority allow that entity to then trade in that jurisdiction without sanction? These are questions which remain unanswered but I hope that in highlighting the difficulties that might be encountered in other international comparative regimes I have alerted the reader to the potential for difficulties. To be forewarned is to be forearmed and any contemplated international business that engages that State's data protection regime should be carefully scrutinised in advance.

The global economy is here to stay. However, the lack of a unified philosophical approach to data protection and regulation will be a serious hindrance to its development. So long as nation states decree that your information is their sovereign property and that data philosophies diverge as to the weight to be given to individual rights, there can be no uniformity in global data regulation. This does not mean business cannot be done outside of the GDPR regime; it may be certainly be possible, but that possibility and the associated risks should be carefully assessed before proceeding.

3.5 INTRUSION DETECTION SYSTEMS EVALUATION GUIDE

AlienVault®

SUMMARY

Intrusion Detection Systems (IDS) have been a mainstay in the security practitioner's arsenal for many years. They are designed to gather and analyse information from networks and hosts to identify possible security breaches. The following guide provides a useful reference for evaluating IDS tools.

Additionally, you'll learn how the AlienVault Unified Security Management® (USM™) platform delivers critical IDS functionality as one of five built-in essential security capabilities. Managed from a single console, AlienVault USM integrates IDS with asset discovery, vulnerability assessment, behavioural monitoring, Security Information and Event Management (SIEM), and real-time threat intelligence from the AlienVault Open Threat Exchange® (OTX™), to add critical context to alarms and give you the ability to quickly detect and respond to threats.

INTRODUCTION

In this guide we will examine the critical components of host and network IDS, and explain how to evaluate IDS solutions.

The core functionalities of network IDS include:

* Monitoring and analysing network and system activities;

* Recognising typical attack patterns; and

* Analysing abnormal network activity patterns.

The core functionalities of host IDS include:

- Analysing system configurations and vulnerabilities;

- Assessing system and file integrity;

- Analysing abnormal user activity patterns; and

- Tracking user policy violations.

Traditional IDS has been around for many years and forms the backbone of any good security practice. But in recent years it has become apparent that the traditional capabilities of IDS are not sufficient to deliver a complete security solution. IDS as a standalone tool provides too narrow a view of the threat vectors facing your organisation. Intrusion detection needs to be augmented with other security capabilities to achieve effective threat detection and response.

Security teams are typically overstressed and under-resourced trying to stay ahead of the evolving threat landscape, and often do not have the time to wade through mountains of alerts. Organisations need an IDS solution that can prioritise alerts and provide a level of context to each one. Receiving an alert in the context of your entire infrastructure allows you to focus your time on addressing the real threats. In addition, threat intelligence is another crucial component to augment the effectiveness of your IDS solution. Threat intelligence is information about malicious actors, their tools, infrastructure and methods. Effective threat intelligence is essential for making sense of mountains of internal and external threat data to enable efficient threat detection and prioritised response. If you can find a solution that includes these key capabilities, you are well on your way to an effective security programme.

The following are the key questions you need to ask when evaluating an IDS solution:

- Does it have both Network Intrusion Detection Systems (NIDS) and Host Intrusion Detection Systems (HIDS)?

- Does the IDS use a signature-based approach?

- What is the throughput of the IDS?

- Does the IDS perform protocol analysis?

- Does the IDS do aggregation (i.e. combining alerts)?

- Does the IDS have integration capabilities (e.g. with other platforms)?

- Does the IDS have contextual enhancement? Does it feed into SIEM?

- How quickly is the IDS able to detect the latest threats via new updates?

NETWORK IDS OR HOST IDS

The first thing you need to determine is if you need a Host-based Intrusion Detection System (HIDS) or a Network-based Intrusion Detection (NIDS) system. Intrusion detection traditionally includes both of these components, and both are essential for a complete security solution.

NIDS

Network-based IDS perform an analysis of all traffic passing through the network and matches the traffic to the library of known attacks. An alert is sent to the administrator when a match to a known attack occurs or if abnormal behavior is identified.

The advantage of network-based IDS solutions is that they can monitor an entire network with only a few well-situated nodes or devices, and they impose little overhead on a network. One disadvantage of Network-based IDS solutions is that the devices have trouble monitoring high-volume traffic. When the traffic volume exceeds the IDS's capabilities, the solution will start dropping packets,[1] causing it to miss attacks launched during peak traffic periods.

HIDS

A Host-based IDS monitors individual hosts on your network for malicious activity.

The Host IDS takes a snapshot of your existing system key files and applications and matches it to the previous snapshot. If the critical system files were modified or deleted, an alert is sent to the administrator to investigate. This functionality is also known as file integrity monitoring.

The advantage of HIDS is that these systems in general tend to be more accurate than Network-based IDS because they analyse the server's log files, not just network traffic patterns. Host-based IDS can analyse activities on the host in a very detailed manner. It can often determine which processes and/or users are involved in malicious activities, and can tell you when an attack has potentially succeeded. The issue with host-based systems is that they tend to be expensive and resource-intensive because they require installing an agent on each host you wish to monitor, with licensing generally charged on a per-seat basis.

---

1. Refer also to the discussion of throughput in the 'Throughput' section below.

Solution recommendations

For a truly effective security control strategy, both NIDS and HIDS are needed for an intrusion detection solution.

NIDS and HIDS complement each other, and each provide functionality that enhances the effectiveness of the other by providing visibility into all traffic on the network as well as traffic targeting each monitored host.

AlienVault USM capabilities

AlienVault Unified Security Management (USM) provides both Network IDS and Host IDS functionality. With AlienVault USM, the Host IDS is simple to set up and comes integrated out-of-the box with Network IDS and a score of additional built-in security tools, all managed from a single console, enabling rapid correlation of events, threats detection, and response prioritisation.

Overview

You need to determine if you want an IDS solution that is signature-based or anomaly-based. There are advantages and disadvantages of both.

Signature-based detection

Signature detection, also known as pattern matching, involves searching network traffic for packet sequences (such as file hashes) that are known to be malicious. Once a match to a signature is found, the system generates an alert.

A key advantage of signature-based IDS is that signatures are easy to develop and understand. In addition, pattern matching can be performed very quickly.

But there are certain limitations of this method. Because the signature can only detect known attacks, some approaches to signature-based detection require the creation of a signature for every attack, and thus previously unseen attacks cannot be detected. In addition, signature engines are prone to false positives because some normal network activity can be misinterpreted as malicious. However, there are ways to mitigate these disadvantages, such as using a strong correlation engine. Correlation engines detect relationships between different types of events to identify malicious activity. In doing so, correlation engines turn disparate data into actionable information.

Anomaly-based detection

Anomaly-based detection incorporates the concept of a baseline for normal network behavior. Events in an anomaly detection engine are identified by any behaviours that fall outside of the predefined or accepted model of behaviour.

One advantage of anomaly-based detection is that a new attack for which a signature does not exist can be detected if the behaviour falls out of the normal traffic patterns. A disadvantage of anomaly-based detection engines is the difficulty of defining rules, as the rules need to be tested extensively for accuracy, and without entering good baseline knowledge of your network, they can generate many false positives. In addition, anomaly detection engines have difficulty translating easily across differing security vendor platforms.

Solution recommendations

Signature-based IDS solutions are the most practical given the resource limitations of most organisations, and one of the most effective solutions for short-term threat detection. For signature-based solutions, you need to look for a solution that rapidly updates signatures when new vulnerabilities and exploits are discovered. The signatures should be updated frequently to ensure they can detect the latest threats as well as reduce false positive alerts. The solution also needs to have the ability to import signatures from commercial and open-source signature feed providers.

AlienVault USM capabilities

AlienVault USM delivers IDS using the signature-based detection method, and the signatures are updated several times a week by the AlienVault Labs threat research team. The USM platform overcomes the traditional shortcomings of the signature-based method with its strong correlation engine. Leveraging the numerous security controls built into the USM platform, the AlienVault correlation engine uses built-in correlation rules to detect relationships between different types of events occurring in one or more monitored assets to identify threats. The use of multiple data sources greatly enhances USM's capability to identify malicious activity. In addition, AlienVault USM integrates Threat Intelligence powered by the Open Threat Exchange (OTX) into the platform, which provides additional context to the IDS engine and delivers signatures on the latest exploits.

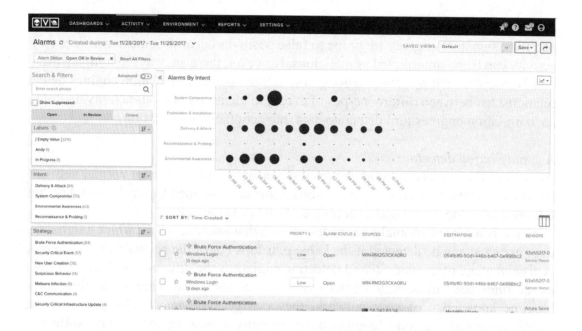

THROUGHPUT

Overview

The next thing to understand about your IDS solution is throughput. Throughput is the maximum amount of traffic that can be successfully processed in one second by the Network IDS system. Your NIDS must be able to keep up with your network traffic. This will largely depend upon your network requirements. Every organization has different bandwidth needs. Typically, the range of 100 Mbps to 1 Gbps is sufficient for most networks. (It is important to remember that networks are full-duplex, meaning a 100 Mbps link can generate 200 Mbps of traffic).

Note that one concern of IDS deployments is the performance factor. Many NIDS implementations have a tendency to drop packets due to the high throughput of today's high bandwidth network devices. Therefore, you must determine where you will put the Network IDS, and how much bandwidth you'll need.

Solution recommendations

Determine your network requirements (i.e. understand what applications you are running, how much bandwidth each application is using, how many users your network is supporting, etc.) and select a NIDS solution that can keep up with your network traffic.

AlienVault USM capabilities

AlienVault USM provides enough throughput for most typical organisations. The NIDS throughput of the AlienVault USM All-in-Ones (AIO) appliances is 100 Mbps, while the throughput of the AlienVault USM Sensors ranges from 100 Mbps for Remote Sensors to 5 Gbps for Enterprise Sensors.

PROTOCOL ANALYSIS

Overview

The next thing to evaluate in your IDS solution is the level of protocol analysis that it performs. In protocol analysis, the Network IDS examines Transmission Control Protocol (TCP) and User Diagram Protocol (UDP) payloads, which contain other protocols such as DNS, FTP, HTTP and SMTP (i.e. the Layer 7 applications). As an example, threats can be transmitted through legitimate DNS traffic, which isn't normally inspected or blocked. The IDS understands how these protocols are supposed to work, and can fully decode and interpret the protocols to detect threats using signatures. This process allows a much larger range of signatures to be created than would be possible through more basic signature techniques.

Solution recommendations

Make sure your IDS solution does robust protocol analysis, including application layer decoding of HTTP, FTP, SMTP, SSL, SSH and DNS protocols.

AlienVault USM capabilities

AlienVault USM performs protocol analysis to deliver an extensive range of signatures.

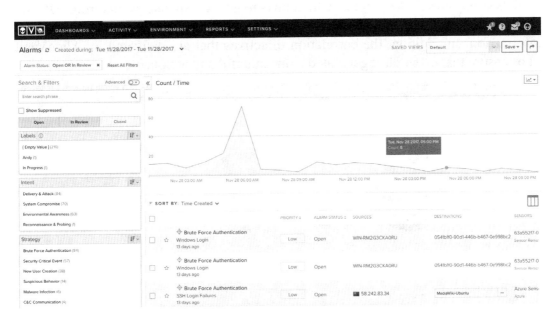

AGGREGATION

Overview

IDS systems generate an enormous amount of data, including scores of alerts and events based upon the signatures in the system. Often there are duplicative events from various systems, and other alerts that could be characterised as noise. This is a major pain point for all organisations – you get flooded with alerts. This can also lead to inadvisable workarounds, including restricting or turning off the signatures altogether. These workarounds are not advisable for multiple reasons. First, an attack may in fact be happening, and you need to be able to properly identify it. In addition, you will lose capabilities that are needed for reporting purposes.

The optimal way to deal with this pain point is to use an IDS solution that has aggregation capabilities. Aggregation, the ability to combine events into one alert, is critical to help you focus your efforts on detecting actual threats. You need to be able to correlate the output of several systems and give your security operators a condensed view of the reported security issues.

Solution recommendations

Select an IDS solution that has aggregation capabilities.

AlienVault USM capabilities

AlienVault USM delivers cutting edge aggregation functionality. It accomplishes this with its strong correlation engine, which links together disparate events from IDS and other built-in security controls to consolidate event data and turn the data into useful information. In addition, the correlation directives that are delivered by AlienVault Labs ensure that every alert generated is meaningful and actionable.

INTEGRATION

Overview

As critical as IDS is to your security program, one security tool is not sufficient. Most companies have multiple security tools to achieve effective threat detection and response. To get the most out of your IDS, it needs to be integrated with other security tools. This means that it needs to have the capability to send and receive alert data to and from other data sources so that you achieve better context and correlation of threat data and better prioritisation of alerts.

Solution recommendations

Choose an IDS solution that has strong integration capabilities.

AlienVault USM capabilities

AlienVault USM was built to integrate data with other platforms, and deliver exceptional correlation capabilities. It is an intuitive, comprehensive security platform that integrates seamlessly with external security tools, in addition to the built-in integration of IDS with asset discovery, vulnerability assessment, behavioural monitoring, and SIEM capabilities. With AlienVault USM, you'll have the ability to incorporate data from 3rd party technologies and devices to better correlate network activity and identify malicious activity. This data feeds into AlienVault USM's correlation engine to greatly enhance threat detection and response capabilities.

CONTEXTUAL ENHANCEMENT

Overview

An IDS on its own can only do so much; IDS data needs to be supplemented with additional data about the network, applications, devices, and users to be really meaningful. The way to do this is with context. Putting threats in context is essential for a truly effective IDS solution. This requires correlating information from a range of sources, including information from internal sources such as NIDS, HIDS, system logs, firewall logs, etc., as well as from external sources. This correlation capability is a must-have for a successful security program.

An effective IDS system also needs to feed into a Security Information and Event Management (SIEM) solution. SIEM software is designed to import information from various security-related logs, including those from IDS, vulnerability assessment, and asset management tools, and to correlate events among them. Integration with SIEM provides additional needed context for your alerts.

Solution recommendations

You need to select an IDS solution with the ability to deliver supplemental data about your hosts to provide additional context to the alerts. This will improve the efficiency and effectiveness of your threat detection capabilities.

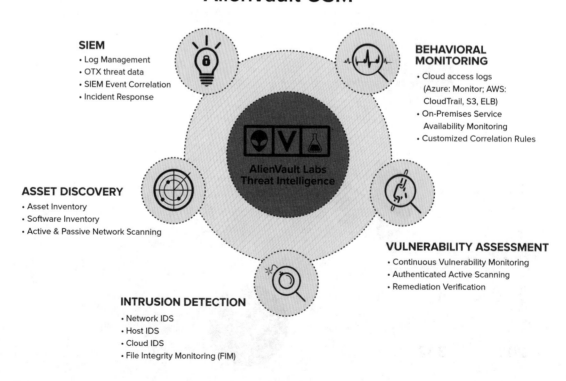

AlienVault USM™

SIEM
- Log Management
- OTX threat data
- SIEM Event Correlation
- Incident Response

BEHAVIORAL MONITORING
- Cloud access logs (Azure: Monitor; AWS: CloudTrail, S3, ELB)
- On-Premises Service Availability Monitoring
- Customized Correlation Rules

AlienVault Labs Threat Intelligence

ASSET DISCOVERY
- Asset Inventory
- Software Inventory
- Active & Passive Network Scanning

VULNERABILITY ASSESSMENT
- Continuous Vulnerability Monitoring
- Authenticated Active Scanning
- Remediation Verification

INTRUSION DETECTION
- Network IDS
- Host IDS
- Cloud IDS
- File Integrity Monitoring (FIM)

AlienVault USM capabilities

AlienVault USM delivers essential security capabilities on top of its IDS in a single platform. The IDS functionality is integrated with asset discovery, vulnerability assessment, and behavioural monitoring in a native SIEM solution to provide critical context. The Threat Intelligence powered by OTX and delivered by AlienVault Labs provides additional context to your alerts, in addition to the coordinated set of rules delivered to the USM platform by the Labs team. The constant updates from AlienVault Labs enable the AlienVault USM platform to analyse the mountain of event data from all of your data sources. Over 2,500 correlation directives link events to identify threats targeting your network, eliminating the need for you to spend hours creating your own. The USM platform delivers a prioritised assessment of the threats targeting your network, telling you the most important threats to focus on right now, and provides guidance on how to respond to those threats.

SUMMARY

Intrusion Detection Systems are one of the most effective security controls available today, particularly when IDS data can be correlated with asset information, vulnerability data, and threat intelligence to provide valuable context and prioritisation of alarms. Using the information in the guide above, you'll be able to effectively assess the capabilities of the many IDS tools available and find the solution that best fits your needs.

AlienVault Unified Security Management Overview

AlienVault's Unified Security Management (USM) platform, described in Chapters 4.2, and 4.3, provides a fast and cost-effective way for organisations with limited security staff and budget to address compliance and threat management needs. With all of the essential security controls built in, AlienVault USM puts complete security visibility within fast and easy reach of smaller security teams, who need to do more with less.

Part Four

Innovative Tools for Cyber Threat Response

4.1 IDENTIFYING AFFORDABLE AND COST-EFFECTIVE SECURITY SOLUTIONS FOR SMES

Nick Ioannou, Boolean Logical Ltd

The reality we currently face is that a large number of small and medium sized businesses do not spend anywhere near enough money on their security solutions to provide adequate protection, or do not spend their money wisely, using up the bulk of their security budget purchasing expensive enterprise grade solutions covering a particular aspect of cyber security. Either way, both scenarios leave gaps that can lead to major business disruption through a breach or malware infection. Some businesses actually go bust within six months after the disruption of a major malware infection, so the importance of cost-effective security has never been higher.

It doesn't matter if you have invested in an expensive AI based behavioural monitoring system, if your defences are easily circumvented. Sure, you know you've been infected or compromised very quickly, but the point is that you have been infected or compromised in the first place. It's a bit like paying for security cameras and a security guard in your house, but not investing in any locks. Likewise, relying on the basic free protection that comes with an operating system is a false economy, as a malware infection like ransomware could cost you dearly if no one can work for 2-3 days, together with the additional cost of removing the infection and recovering your data. It is important that small businesses get out of the mindset that they have nothing of value to protect that the cyber criminals would be interested in, so do not need to invest in security the same way larger firms would. The vast opportunities for extortion and unauthorised use of your infrastructure or assets and the disruption it would cause is enough to justify spending money on security. There are also a lot of things that can be done that do not have any costs other than someone's time, like the removal of admin rights for standard users, using OpenDNS or creating rules to block obscure email file attachments that you know no one will ever send you other than a cyber criminal.

When it comes to evaluating the costs of a security solution, it is worth bearing in mind that many vendors offer discounts like 3 year subscriptions for the price of 2 years or competitor cross-grade pricing. It is worth asking and getting multiple quotes from channel partners who get incentives from the security solution vendors. I always ask if there are prices tiers or bands to check if I'm close to the next tier with the number of users, because sometimes 51 users costs the roughly the same as 48 due to flat discounts applied to the next tier. Price is only one factor to consider though; function and performance also need to be factored in. Sometimes a secondary function of one product can be more cost-effective than a product that has that as its main function, albeit not as good, but better than not having it at all. The phrase I always use when speaking at conferences is that I am looking for the 'VW Golf sweet spot for value, performance and function.' As much I would like a Mercedes E class or a Maserati, I cannot justify it to the business. Also, knowing what you need something for is a great help in steering you to the right solution. To be protected, SMEs need to make sure the following six key areas are covered: Antivirus, Patch management, Email filtering, Web filtering, Admin privilege management and Access control. An additional two areas complete the circle, with Monitoring, Forensics and Remediation. That said, there is one more area which needs its own circle, which is backups, because if your security defences fail or are compromised, it is your backups that you turn to. We will assume, though, that a robust backup regime is in place, as it is often funded via the disaster recovery and business continuity budgets for most businesses and focus on the other areas of security.

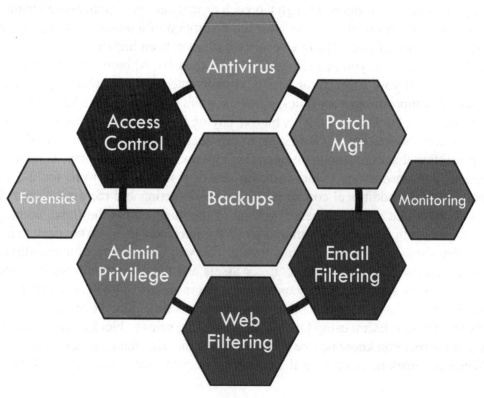

So for antivirus or endpoint security, there is a wide array of solutions available, but I prefer combined solutions with patch/update management included, which narrows my choices quite considerably. The way I see it, unpatched security vulnerabilities can make your security solution next to worthless, so rather than rely on a separate patch/update management system, a combined system can be more cost-effective and more efficient, as one dashboard gives you an overview of both the security and patch status of your computers. I also prefer the admin side to be a cloud based solution, which means there is no box in the corner running the show that everyone needs to connect to, whether it is an additional new server or installed on an existing server. Colleagues who are never in the office are no different to those that are, as the updates and reporting is done over the computer's internet connection, without the need for a VPN connection. Given my criteria of a combined cloud based desktop antivirus and patch management system, the solution I finally decided on was the F-Secure Protection Service for Business, with an annual cost per head of less than £20 on a 3 year subscription.

Setting up an F-Secure management portal account is the first step, from which you can either send colleagues an email with an installation link that includes the embedded activation code, or you can manually download the installer. Once in-stalled, the user's computer appears on the management portal dashboard and you quickly get an insight into your security status. For me, a high number of systems had patches missing on quite obscure software and freeware utilities. This was despite moving from another patch management system that clearly wasn't anywhere near as thorough. One of the advantages of a patch management system is that it identifies software which you may not have expected to be installed on colleagues' machines, as well as software you thought had been removed ages ago. You can then decide on the best course of action to either remove or update the software concerned. If the unexpected software installed turns out to be an illegal 'cracked' copy, remove it and run a deep malware scan as many of the key generator or 'crack' utilities used to bypass the licensing mechanism are often viruses as well.

I know a lot of small businesses rely on free or home user antivirus software on their computers, often using a selection of products depending on what came pre-installed with the computer. This results in a mixture of protection expiry dates and software versions in the case of home user antivirus, together with no central reporting if something is flagged as suspicious by the software. Antivirus subscription renewal dates can easily be missed, leaving users with limited protection and this can be for months before anyone gets around to sorting it. Worse still is that in many cases, the built-in free basic antivirus is totally disabled, which ironically could offer greater protection than the paid for but expired software. Also, renewing home user antivirus via its renewal prompt directly with the manufacturer is often the most expensive way to extend a subscription, sometimes costing more than double the available retail price. Many people think that business antivirus is more expensive, but in most cases the opposite is true.

The management portal is what sets apart business antivirus and a cloud based portal allows you to be anywhere, on practically any device, and still be able to administer the security solution. I always advise purchasing an extra 5-10% subscriptions than you need, to allow for new staff, or new computer system deployments where there is an overlap and unexpected computer purchases. Not having enough licences because two directors decided they wanted new Microsoft Surface Pros and bought them on the weekend themselves, or a similar scenario, is something that happens in most SMEs, so pre-empting it is probably wise. From the management portal you can also see which users rarely turn on a second machine like a laptop, as the last update time is reported. Machines that are powered off for weeks or months at a time can be a security risk when they are first used again, as system security updates will be missing and prompts to install patches are often ignored. Logically the reason they are powered up and brought back into use will probably be to meet a work deadline, so losing an hour waiting for updates isn't viable. So using the dashboard update history, it is worth asking affected users to turn on and connect those machines before it becomes an issue.

Remember the six key areas I mentioned earlier that need to be covered, which were Antivirus, Patch management, Email filtering, Web filtering, Admin privilege management and Access control. F-Secure Protection Service for Business covers the first four quite well and if combined with additional cloud based email and web filtering, will give you a high degree of protection. Though don't just take my word for it, as F-Secure Protection Service for Business won Best SMB Security Product at the 2016 V3 Technology Awards. I was already six months into my F-Secure subscription when the award was announced. Alternatively, Heimdal CORP is another combined antivirus and patch management system that is worth considering and if you prefer to keep your patch management separate, Ninite Pro is a very cost-effective cloud based solution at only $35 a month in total for 50 machines. There are good security solutions available – the hardest bit is finding out about them before you sign up for something else. Talking to peers at conferences and industry events is one of the best ways to find out about different solutions and recommendations. It is important to set a realistic security budget based on how much you are comfortable spending per person per month. If you focus on the total spend you often end up cost cutting because the figures seem large, but by focusing on the per person costs it puts it into context. It costs me roughly £4.50 a week for all my firm's eight security solutions, or £22 a month, which is £240 a year, with a total spend of £8,500. Admin privilege management at its most basic level of removing admin rights from standard users has no software cost as such, but raises everyone's security levels. Privilege management systems can be expensive, though the cloud based CyberArk solution I signed up for turned out to be £21 per person per year, whereas I nearly signed up for a system where the annual 20% maintenance subscription was close to this figure. Access control at its lowest level can just be good password policies and network permissions, all the way up to multi-factor authentication systems.

In summary, by covering the six key areas within your accepted budget you can find cost-effective security to protect your business from the disruption of a major malware infection. Just remember to set a realistic per person budget and shop around. There is no point spending the entire budget on one area, no matter how good it is, leaving the other five areas empty. There is no excuse to leave any areas empty, just make sure you have something in place, otherwise the cyber criminals will thank you.

4.2 DETECTING RANSOMWARE WITH UNIFIED SECURITY MANAGEMENT®

AlienVault®

INTRODUCTION – REDUCE YOUR RISK OF EXTORTION

In a recent ransomware survey, 80% of respondents perceived ransomware as an extreme or moderate threat, and of those organisations who suffered a ransomware attack, 75% experienced up to five attacks over one year.[1] It's no surprise given that ransomware is (as of writing) a US$2 billion 'market', and rapidly growing as threat actors including organised crime and malicious states try to take their share.[2]

Threat detection or threat monitoring tools provide a critical layer of defence against ransomware attacks. Real-time detection and rapid response is crucial to your ability to contain a ransomware outbreak and to limit its impact. This extends to everywhere you've deployed assets, whether on-premises, in public clouds such as Microsoft Azure or Amazon Web Services, or in cloud applications like Microsoft Office 365 and Google G Suite.

AlienVault® Unified Security Management® (USM) delivers three critical success factors for combating ransomware attacks against all of your critical infrastructure. First, AlienVault USM provides you with the essential security capabilities you need to quickly detect and contain ransomware attacks across your cloud and on-premises environments. Second, continuously updated threat intelligence from the AlienVault Labs Security Research Team and the Open Threat Exchange® (OTX™) ensures the USM platform is always up to date with the knowledge required to detect

---

1. 2017 Ransomware Report, Cybersecurity Insiders, https://www.alienvault.com/resource-center/analyst-reports/2017-ransomware-report

2. Ransomware Payments to Hit a Record $2 Billion in 2017: Research, LIFARS (Nov 2017), https://lifars.com/2017/11/ransomware-payments-hit-record-2-billion-2017-research

emerging ransomware tools and techniques, and ensures that you have the context needed to understand the threat and how to respond. Thirdly, AlienVault USM delivers integrated security automation and orchestrated response capabilities where you can manually or automatically respond to detected threats using other IT security and operations products, such as working with Carbon Black to isolate a system infected by ransomware.

HOW RANSOMWARE WORKS

Employees are the weakest link when it comes to ransomware, which often infiltrates organisations via infected email attachments, phishing emails, or by visiting malicious or compromised websites. While these attack methods remain popular, they are not the only distribution method of ransomware. In May 2017, a massive global ransomware outbreak known as WannaCry was propagated by exploiting a vulnerability in the SMB (Server Message Block) service of unpatched Microsoft Windows operating systems. What made it worse is that it was one of the first ransomware variants that was a work type of malware, meaning that the ransomware attempted to self-propagate itself to other vulnerable systems. Since that attack, other ransomware variants have emerged, many of which have leveraged the NSA-developed attack methods leaked by a group of malicious actors known as the Shadow Brokers group.

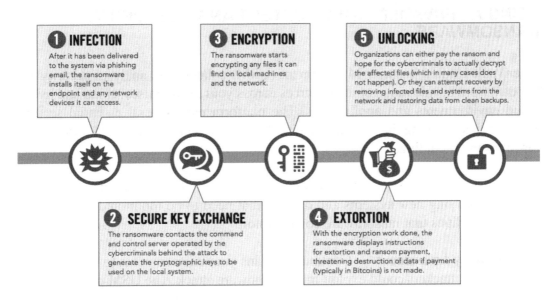

Anatomy of a Ransomware Attack[3]

---

3. 2017 Ransomware Report, Cybersecurity Insiders: https://www.alienvault.com/resource-center/analyst-reports/2017-ransomware-report

Historically, ransomware has primarily targeted Windows operating systems, though Linux and Mac OS X variants are becoming more prevalent. The most well-known type of ransomware is one that encrypts specific files, rendering the system or specific data unusable. This type of encrypting ransomware typically, once the malicious file executes, connects to a Command and Control (C&C, or C2) server to either notify the attacker of its successful infection of a system, gain further instructions, or obtain an encryption key. It then begins to encrypt files on the victim's system as well as any shared drives. The ransomware then displays a ransom note, demanding payment in exchange for a key to decrypt the files. With ransomware using modern encryption algorithms, like AES or RSA, it makes it nearly impossible to guess or crack the key.

In many cases, outbound communication from an infected system is difficult to detect due to ransomware employing techniques such as domain generation algorithms (DGAs). The DGA algorithm enables the ransomware administrator to create thousands of random domains every day that it can use for one or more C&C servers. The same algorithm running on each infected system generates that same list of random domains, and the ransomware tries to connect to each of those domains until it successfully connects to a target C&C server. This approach makes it challenging to use traditional defence tactics like a blacklist to block the connection to a known malicious IP address or domain.

USING ALIENVAULT USM TO DETECT AND RESPOND TO RANSOMWARE

AlienVault Unified Security Management (USM) collects and analyses security and log data from a wide range of data sources across your on-premises, cloud and hybrid cloud environments and applications. The platform uses several essential security technologies working in concert to detect and respond to advanced threats like ransomware, including:

Asset Discovery — Monitors your on-premises and cloud environments for new assets, identifying new systems and devices that need to be monitored and assessed for vulnerabilities that ransomware could exploit.

Vulnerability Assessment — Continually scans your environments to detect vulnerabilities that attackers could exploit in a ransomware attack. The USM platform ranks vulnerabilities by severity so that you can prioritise your remediation efforts.

Network Intrusion Detection (IDS) — Analyses the network traffic to detect signatures of known ransomware, and communications with known malicious servers. Using field-proven IDS technologies, AlienVault USM identifies attacks, malware, policy violations and port scans that could be indicators of malicious activity on your networks.

Host Intrusion Detection (HIDS) and File Integrity Monitoring (FIM) — Analyzes system behavior and configuration status to identify suspicious activity and potential exposure. This includes the ability to identify changes to critical system and application files, as well as modifications to the Windows Registry, that could be made to initiate the ransomware's encryption engine.

SIEM Event Correlation — Using machine learning and state-based correlation, the USM platform analyses a large number of seemingly unrelated events across disparate systems to pinpoint the few events that are truly important in that mass of information. The AlienVault Labs Threat Research Team regularly updates the USM platform with ransomware-specific correlation rules that identify a range of behaviors that are indicative of a ransomware infection, including downloading the ransomware file, systems attempting to connect with a C&C server and post data, multiple failed connections from a system attempting to connect to a domain (or multiple domains) within a narrow time window, and more.

SIEM Log Management & Reporting — The USM platform provides the ability to automate the centralised collection and normalisation of events and logs from devices, servers, applications and more from across your on-premises and cloud environments, as well as from your cloud applications like Office 365. This data is centrally retained for at least one year, helping support compliance requirements and the ability to perform forensics on attacks that may have only recently been discovered, but that require investigation of more historic data. Centralising collection also supports the automatic analysis of anomalies and attacks like ransomware, and enables analysts to perform search and forensics on collected data. Analysts can also run any of the built-in and customisable reports, so as to demonstrate compliance with standards like PCI DSS, or for regular reviews of security events and activities.

ALIENVAULT THREAT INTELLIGENCE

Cyber criminals and attackers are constantly adapting their methods, making for a constantly evolving threat landscape. Most organisations don't have the time or resources to research the threat environment and continuously update their detection capabilities based on new and emerging threats. The AlienVault Labs Security Research Team handles this task on behalf of AlienVault USM users by delivering continuous threat intelligence updates to the USM platform to keep the threat detection capabilities up to date with the latest threats.

In fact, for many recent threats, the threat detection capabilities were updated the same day, or even *before* specific vulnerabilities were exploited.

THREAT	DISCOVERED	THREAT DETECTION CAPABILITIES UPDATED IN ALIENVAULT USM
"Petya" / NotPetya	June 27, 2017	Same day
WannaCry	May 12, 2017	Same day
Samba CVE-2017-7494	May 25, 2017	Same day
WordPress Content Injection	February 1, 2017	6 days BEFORE
Adobe 0-day (CVE-2015-0311)	January 22, 2015	3 months BEFORE

Threat intelligence integrated into the USM platform eliminates the need for IT teams to spend time or resources conducting their own research on emerging threats. This threat intelligence is continuously updated in response to new and updated threats, meaning that essential rule sets and threat information are readily available to detect the latest threats, including:

- Correlation directives – translates raw events into actionable remediation tasks;

- Network and host IDS signatures – detects the latest threats in your environment;

- Asset discovery signatures – identifies the latest OSs, applications and device types;

- Vulnerability assessment signatures – finds the latest vulnerabilities on all your systems;

- Report templates – provides new ways of viewing data about your environment and / or meeting compliance requirements;

- Dynamic incident response templates – delivers customised guidance on how to respond to each alert; and

- Support for new data sources – expands your monitoring footprint.

The AlienVault Labs team also utilises the power of the AlienVault Open Threat Exchange (OTX). OTX is the world's first truly open threat intelligence community that enables collaborative research. This global community of over 65,000 subscribers, including security researchers and practitioners, contributes over 14 million real-time threat data artifacts to OTX every day. This includes information about ransomware outbreaks as they emerge in the wild, including Indicators of Compromise (IoCs), details about threat actors, targeted industries, and more. OTX enables everyone in the OTX community to share threat data, strengthening their own defences while helping others do the same.

OTX is fully integrated with AlienVault USM, so you get additional insight into malicious activity targeting your network. This integration with OTX enables AlienVault USM to quickly identify indicators of attacks previously reported by other members of OTX.

REDUCE THE TIME BETWEEN DETECTION AND RESPONSE WITH SECURITY ORCHESTRATION & AUTOMATION

A ransomware attack can spread rapidly across your systems and quickly render them unusable. Time is of the essence. As soon as ransomware is detected in your environment, you must move swiftly to contain the threat and to prevent it from proliferating across your environment. If done manually or done across many disparate systems, or if the attack happens outside of typical working hours, your response effort may be delayed or too slow to contain the attack.

AlienVault USM has advanced security orchestration and automation capabilities that help you respond quickly and efficiently to threats affecting your environments, including response actions that work in alignment with third-party security tools like Cisco Umbrella, Palo Alto Networks, and Carbon Black. For example, if the USM platform detects evidence of ransomware on one of your assets, you can easily orchestrate the isolation of that system from your network via the built-in integration with Carbon Black, helping to prevent further spread of the ransomware.

The security orchestration responses available within AlienVault USM can also be automated, making your response faster and more efficient. For example, if AlienVault USM detects communication with a DGA-generated domain known to be malicious, such as ransomware communicating with its 'Command & Control' server, you can orchestrate a response action that passes the malicious domain details to Cisco Umbrella, which then blocks traffic between that domain and your employees and assets.

DECREASING YOUR RISK FROM RANSOMWARE

Ransomware is a prevalent threat, and the industry expects to see an increased frequency of attacks in the coming years. While not knowing when the next ransomware attack will hit, or what methods it will use, there are several steps you can put into practice to decrease your risk from ransomware:

- **Architect your environment to minimize cross-infection** – This includes implementing network segmentation, and a least-privilege model, to limit ability for any ransomware to traverse the network.

- **Implement a backup plan** – Even if only part of your data is irretrievably lost due to a ransomware attack, it can still cost your organisation in terms of lost productivity and the efforts to try to retrieve that data. Defining and implementing a backup policy is a critical defence, and in particular using offline backups.

- **Train your organisation** – People are often the weak link when it comes to ransomware. Regularly train your employees on how to watch for phishing attempts, the risks associated with opening email attachments, and more. Equally important is to ensure they know what to do if they feel that they have been compromised, including who and how to report the incident to ensure the fastest response.

- **Regularly scan for and patch vulnerabilities** – The WannaCry ransomware took advantage of an exploit for which a patch had been available for over one month, and those organisations impacted were either unaware of the patch or had failed to deploy the patch in a timely fashion. Knowing what assets exist across your environment, what software and services they run, understanding where vulnerabilities exist and what patches are available is critical to being able to shore up any gaps before a malicious actor is able to design an attack that can take advantage of that vulnerability.

- **Ensure your security solution(s) are up to date** – Any software solution may have flaws, and many software security solutions like vulnerability or malware defense solutions require threat intelligence to be able to know what threats are out there and how to detect them. Ensure that you regularly update your security solutions to address any issues, add new and enhanced capabilities, and ensure that they are running with their latest threat intelligence so that they are optimally protecting your environment.

In addition, you should deploy security essentials including asset discovery, vulnerability assessment, intrusion detection, behavioral monitoring, SIEM correlation and log management. However, deploying traditional security point-products requires extensive configuration and tuning during deployment and monitoring after deployment. The lack of integration with other tools means that even with a centralised management console like a SIEM, IT teams have to dedicate a significant amount of staff time to managing each security control and even more time trying to consolidate and correlate all of the alerts being generated by those tools.

This is where AlienVault USM offers an affordable yet comprehensive solution in your battle against ransomware and other threats. It provides built-in essential security capabilities in a unified solution, integrating threat intelligence from AlienVault Labs and OTX, and delivers security orchestration and automation for efficient incident response.

The USM platform provides an effective defence against ransomware and other attacks in a solution that significantly reduces complexity and deployment time, and where you can go from installation to first insight in as little as one hour.

Next Steps:

- Take AlienVault USM for a test drive in our on-line demo environment.

- Start detecting threats in your environment today with a free trial.

- View pricing and request a quote.

4.3 PETYA RANSOMWARE RAPID RESPONSE GUIDE

AlienVault®

THE NEW WAVE OF GLOBAL RANSOMWARE ATTACKS

On June 27th 2017, security researchers at AlienVault Labs reported seeing a new wave of "Petya"-like ransomware attacks hitting organisations across Ukraine, Russia and the rest of Europe. Targets of the global ransomware campaign included the Ukrainian government, the Chernobyl nuclear radiation monitoring system, U.S. pharmaceutical company Merck, Russian steel and mining firms, and many others[1]. However, the full extent of damage from this latest outbreak continues to unfold.

As with the previous WannaCry ransomware campaign, this latest strain of Petya ransomware exploits the Windows SMB v1 vulnerability on unpatched computers. However, it has the capacity to spread rapidly throughout the network using the Windows PsExec and WMI services, meaning that computers that had previously been patched with MS17-010 are still vulnerable to an attack. Therefore, it's important to understand how this Petya variant works, how to detect an infection in your environment, and how to respond quickly and effectively to stop the infection from spreading throughout your organisation.

WHAT WE KNOW ABOUT THIS RANSOMWARE CAMPAIGN

1. It uses the EternalBlue exploit.
Allegedly developed by the U.S. National Security Agency (NSA) and leaked by the Shadow Brokers hacker group in April 2017, EternalBlue exploits a vulnerability

---

1. https://www.nytimes.com/2017/06/27/technology/global-ransomware-hack-what-we-know-and-dont-know. html?smid=tw-share&_r=0&referer=https://t.co/xYPfx14y8I

(CVE-2017-0144[2]) in Microsoft's Server Message Block (SMB) version 1 protocol, allowing remote attackers to execute code on a target system. While Microsoft issued an update in March 2017, it became apparent during the May 2017 WannaCry outbreak that many systems had not yet been patched.

2. It has not been associated with an email phishing campaign.
Before you send a scathing email reminder to your users to not click on suspicious links, it's important to know that this variant of ransomware has not been associated with an email phishing campaign. While the majority of ransomware attacks are initiated as a Trojan sent through email with an attachment or link directing users to a malicious website for a drive-by malware download, in the case of this attack, the initial infection vector was associated with a software update for a Ukrainian tax accounting program called MeDoc[3], which is popular in Ukraine. This aligns with the fact that Ukraine appeared to be the epicentre of the attacks.

3. It overwrites the Master Boot Record (MBR).
Once it has compromised a system, the ransomware overwrites the Master Boot Record (MBR) and encrypts individual files that match a list of file extensions (including documents, archives, and more). After a reboot of the system, the infected computer is unable to load the typical Windows operating system files, and instead displays a message with instructions for paying a ransom to decrypt the files on the system.

4. The ransom note and code match the Petya ransomware.
Petya first emerged in a 2016 ransomware campaign. It used a new and different approach to ransomware at the time, overwriting the Master Boot Record (MBR) with a customer boot loader to load a malicious kernel that proceeded to encrypt the drive.

5. It spreads using Microsoft PsExec and WMI.
This ransomware variant spreads laterally throughout a network using Microsoft PSExec and WMI. This means that even computers that have been patched are still vulnerable to infection.

PsExec is a Microsoft alternative to a Telnet service used to remotely troubleshoot machines and devices. According to Microsoft[4], PsExec allows you to "execute processes on other systems, complete with full interactivity for console applications, without having to manually install client software." This includes the ability to launch

---

2. https://www.cve.mitre.org/cgi-bin/cvename.cgi?name=CVE-2017-0144

3. http://blog.talosintelligence.com/2017/06/worldwide-ransomware-variant.html?m=1

4. https://technet.microsoft.com/en-us/sysinternals/bb897553.aspx

interactive command-prompt windows on remote devices as well as to use MS-DOS tools like ipconfig, to show information about the device.

STEPS FOR DETECTING AND RESPONDING TO PETYA RANSOMWARE

1. Scan your environment for vulnerabilities

Don't wait for an infection to be detected in your network. Before an intrusion occurs, you should know whether your critical infrastructure has known vulnerabilities in its operating system or applications that could make it susceptible to a ransomware attack, and take steps to remediate those vulnerabilities. In this case, you should run a vulnerability scan of your assets to identify the CVE-2017-0144 Windows vulnerability.

AlienVault USM features a built-in vulnerability assessment capability to assess whether your systems and devices are currently at risk. Because USM receives continuous threat intelligence updates, including the latest vulnerability signatures, USM users have the assurance that their vulnerability scans use the latest known vulnerability signatures.

If vulnerabilities are found in your environment, take swift action to patch your systems, and then re-scan your environment. With USM, you can easily run on-demand vulnerability scans on any part of your environment.

2. Know what services and applications are running on your critical assets.

The latest strain of Petya ransomware leverages flaws in Microsoft's SMB v1 service, a service that may not be required or essential to organisations. For a healthy security posture, maintain an always up-to-date asset inventory that identifies all the services and applications running on critical assets. In doing so, you can identify and disable any non-essential services (like SMB v1) that may expose you to an attack.

AlienVault USM performs continuous asset discovery and inventory. It automatically finds and provides you with visibility into the assets in your on-premises and cloud environments. With AlienVault USM, you can discover all the IP-enabled devices on your network and determine what software and services are installed on them, how they're configured, and whether there are any potential vulnerabilities and active threats being executed against them.

3. Ensure that your critical systems and data are backed up and ready for restore.

If you don't currently take regular backups, consider this Petya ransomware attack a warning shot. Every organisation should have a healthy backup process that includes air-gapped or offline backups, when needed, to restore critical data. Otherwise, the only option for restoring data following a ransomware attack may be to pay the bitcoins ransom, which in itself is no guarantee that you'll be able to decrypt the files on a compromised system.

4. Monitor your environments to detect threats and intrusions.

To prevent malware and ransomware attacks, it's important to ensure that your malware prevention tools, including antivirus and firewalls, are configured properly and are up to date with the latest threat indicators. As a security measure against Petya ransomware, you might consider *blocking ports 445 (SMB) and 139 (file and printer sharing) from any user or entity outside of your organisation.*

However, threat prevention is only one side of the coin. You should also monitor your environment continuously to look for intrusions and threats. AlienVault USM not only centralises and analyses log data from your firewalls and other IPS tools, but it also includes multiple built-in intrusion detection system (IDS) technologies that constantly monitor your environments. This includes network intrusion detection, host intrusion detection, file integrity monitoring, and cloud intrusion detection.

The built-in intrusion detection tools in USM work to identify threats like ransomware and alert users whenever such threats are detected. USM receives continuous threat intelligence updates from the AlienVault Labs Security Research Team and uses the latest global security data in its intrusion detection activities.

As of April 18th, AlienVault USM users benefited from a threat intelligence update that included an IDS signature to detect EternalBlue exploits in their environments. The AlienVault Labs Security Research Team leverages threat data from the Open Threat Exchange (OTX), the world's largest open threat community. During the initial Petya attack outbreak, OTX community members shared their threat data related to the ransomware, creating a Pulse of indicators of compromise (IoCs) to the benefit of the global threat intelligence community—and for the direct benefit of USM users.

OTX is the world's first truly open threat intelligence community that enables collaborative defence with open access and collaborative research. There are over 10 million threat indicators submitted by the community to OTX every day, from over 53,000 participants in over 140 countries. *OTX, where all the Petya indicators of compromise (IoCs) can be viewed, is free to join.*

5. If Petya is detected in your environment, take swift action to isolate the infection.

During a ransomware attack, early detection and response are imperative to stop the attack from spreading across the network. By isolating infected machines quickly, you stand a better chance at preventing a full network shutdown. The steps to mitigate any compromised system on your network are similar for most malware and ransomware threats.

- Isolate the system from your network, to prevent spread of the ransomware to other systems.

- Run forensics and anti-malware software on the infected system, confirming that the anti-malware is running with its latest update. Depending on the severity of the compromise, this may require you to attach the drives of the infected system as external disks, but this should be a last resort.

- Run additional forensics on your network data to better understand the scope of the compromise. You can also search events gathered from across your network and any cloud environments and SaaS services (e.g. Office 365) using a log management tool like USM Anywhere.

- Report the ransomware incident to the respective authority. For example, US organisations should report any incident to the Internet Crime Compliance Center (IC3)[5].

ADVANCED RANSOMWARE DETECTION WITH ALIENVAULT USM

A unified approach to threat detection and response is the most effective way to combat advanced threats like ransomware as it gives you all the threat context you need to detect, investigate, and respond to an emerging threat—all in a single pane of glass. AlienVault USM delivers multiple essential security technologies that work in concert to detect threats like ransomware.

AlienVault USM combines the power of asset discovery, vulnerability assessment, intrusion detection, behavioural monitoring, SIEM, and log management in one unified console, giving you complete security visibility of your on-premises and cloud infrastructure.

The AlienVault USM platform uses a variety of intrusion detection (IDS) technologies and more to gather information on a range of threat vectors to provide the 'who, what, where, when, and how' of these attacks, including:

- **Network Intrusion Detection (IDS) — This** analyses the network traffic to detect signatures of known attacks and patterns that indicate malicious activity. Using field-proven IDS technologies, USM identifies attacks, malware, policy violations, and port scans by performing signature, anomaly, and protocol analysis.

- **Host Intrusion Detection (HIDS) and File Integrity Monitoring (FIM) – This** analyses system behavior and configuration status to identify suspicious activity and potential exposure. This includes the ability to identify the registry change required to initiate the ransomware's encryption engine.

---

5. https://www.ic3.gov/default.aspx

- **Correlation Directives** – The AlienVault Labs Security Research Team regularly adds ransomware-specific correlation directives that identify a range of behaviors that are indicative of a ransomware infection, including:

  * Downloading the ransomware file;
  * Systems attempting to connect with a C&C server and post data; and
  * Multiple failed connections from a system attempting to connect to a domain (or multiple domains) within a narrow time window.

ALIENVAULT LABS THREAT INTELLIGENCE

Cyber criminals and attackers are constantly evolving their methods, making for a constantly evolving threat landscape. Organisations don't have the time or resources to continuously monitor the threat environment. Instead, they turn to MSSPs such as AlienVault to help detect the latest threats. The AlienVault LabsThreat Research team spends countless hours mapping out the different types of attacks, the latest threats, suspicious behavior, vulnerabilities and exploits they uncover across the entire threat landscape.

The AlienVault Labs team regularly delivers threat intelligence as a coordinated set of updates to the USM platform, which accelerates and simplifies threat detection, prioritisation, and response:

- **Correlation directives** – translates raw events into actionable remediation tasks.

- **Network and host IDS signatures** – detects the latest threats in your environment.

- **Asset discovery signatures** – identifies the latest OSs, applications and device types.

- **Vulnerability assessment signatures** – finds the latest vulnerabilities on all your systems.

- **Reporting modules** – provides new ways of viewing data about your environment to meet compliance.

- **Dynamic incident response templates** – delivers customised guidance on how to respond to each alert.

- **Newly supported data source plug-ins** – expands your monitoring footprint.

You also have the ability to export indicators of compromise (IoCs) from OTX to almost any security product. OTX enables everyone in the OTX community to actively collaborate, strengthening their own defences while helping others do the same.

ALIENVAULT UNIFIED SECURITY MANAGEMENT (USM)

As identified in Chapter 4.2, the AlienVault USM platform puts complete security visibility within fast and easy reach of smaller security teams who need to do more with less. USM combines the following essential security capabilities for unified security visibility and management:

- **Asset Discovery and Asset Inventory:** Get visibility into the assets and user activity in your environments.

- **Vulnerability Assessment:** Continuously scan your on-premises and cloud environments to assess vulnerabilities and leverage built-in remediation guidance to prevent those vulnerabilities from being exploited.

- **Intrusion Detection:** Inspect traffic between devices and protect critical assets and systems in your cloud and on-premises environments with multiple intrusion detection technologies in one platform:

  * Network IDS
  * Host IDS
  * File Integrity Monitoring
  * Cloud Intrusion Detection

- **Behavioural Monitoring:** Identify suspicious behavior and potentially compromised systems.

- **SIEM:** Correlate and analyse security event data from across your cloud and on-premises environments.

SUMMARY – ALIENVAULT PRODUCTS

Traditional security point-products require extensive configuration and tuning during deployment, and monitoring after deployment. The lack of integration with other tools means that even with a centralised management console like SIEM, IT teams have to dedicate a significant amount of staff time to managing each security control, and even more time trying to consolidate and correlate all of the alerts being generated by those tools.

By providing built-in essential security capabilities and integrating threat intelligence from AlienVault Labs Security Research Team, AlienVault USM significantly reduces complexity and deployment time so that users can go from installation to first insight in about an hour.

The AlienVault approach delivers a unique solution to the challenge that under-resourced IT teams face when trying to secure their networks. The USM platform, which is a built-in stack of integrated, essential security technologies, is supplemented by the expertise of AlienVault's experienced team of security experts, whose sole job is to analyse changes in the threat landscape. They then create the threat intelligence updates that are delivered regularly as a coordinated set of enhanced detection capabilities, advanced correlation rules and reports, that help AlienVault customers detect, prioritise, and respond to the most critical issues in their networks, such as ransomware.

4.4 THE INCIDENT RESPONSE TOOLKIT: PUTTING THE OODA LOOP TO WORK IN THE REAL WORLD

AlienVault®

When it comes to data breaches, most agree that it's not a matter of if, but when. In a recent report, an astounding 76% of surveyed organizations admitted being victims of successful cyber attacks in 2015 – up from 70% in 2014 and 62% in 2013.

That's why it's so essential to have the right tools in place to spot an event as soon as it happens, as well as be able to respond effectively to minimise damage and recover quickly.

We believe the best way to approach Incident Response is to deploy the OODA Loop method, developed by US Air Force military strategist John Boyd. The OODA Loop focuses on the key essential tactics for responding to any crisis: Observe, Orient, Decide, and Act.

THE ESSENTIAL FACTORS IN INCIDENT RESPONSE

In this chapter, you'll read about a few specific use cases where AlienVault technologies and services help you Observe, Orient, Decide, and Act for effective incident response.

When observing for potential risks and impending threats, there are three essential success factors that should guide your activity as an incident responder, using Security Monitoring to identify anomalous behaviour that may require investigation:

- Observe from all angles.

- Apply prioritisation based on the latest threat intelligence.

- Continuously fine-tune security monitoring tools.

Observe from all angles

AlienVault's Unified Security Management (USM) platform provides the 360-degree view that you need for full situational awareness. By combining and analysing data from native capabilities (e.g. netflow analysis, vulnerability scans, host and network-based IDS) as well as the event logs from your assets, AlienVault USM powers observation from all angles, as described in Chapter 4.3.

Since attackers will probe multiple systems as well as multiple layers of your defences, it's essential that you're constantly observing activity in all of these areas, across all your devices. Additionally, each of these defensive layers should be analysed within a unified context, which is precisely what the AlienVault USM platform gives you.

Apply prioritisation

Emerging AlienVault Labs Threat Intelligence will help you to know when an attack is happening and what you should be looking for. That brings us to Lockheed Martin's Cyber Kill Chain. The Cyber Kill Chain represents the steps that any attacker needs to deploy to compromise a system in order to steal data.

AlienVault has simplified the 7-step Cyber Kill Chain into a 5-step process, based upon AlienVault Labs research into emerging attacker tools, techniques and tactics as described in Chapters 4.3 and 4.4. The AlienVault Labs threat intelligence fuels the USM platform with automated correlation rule analysis using key Indicators of Compromise (IOC) data and automated event classification. The AlienVault Labs team of threat researchers deliver regular updates to USM's built-in security controls.

In order to help you more effectively prioritise each security event, AlienVault USM automatically classifies each event that occurs within your network according to this simplified Cyber Kill Chain. In this way, by automating event analysis and classification, AlienVault USM arms your security team with automated prioritisation for effective incident response.

Continuously fine-tune security monitoring tools

As you discover more about patterns in your network traffic, user activity and service availability statistics, you may want to fine-tune your monitoring tools to ensure that you're capturing all the information you'll need to investigate incidents. Moreover, as new threats emerge, you'll want to make sure that you're checking for these key indicators – such as file checksums or vulnerability signatures.

Each of AlienVault USM's combined security monitoring capabilities can be easily reconfigured – on an individual basis – to give you precisely the observational control you need to detect and stop data breaches.

Examples of how to reconfigure your toolkit
What happened?

- *A new SSL vulnerability has been announced.* What happened? What do you do? First, check your latest vulnerability report to see if any of your assets are vulnerable. Second, evaluate the SSL checks that are enabled within the vulnerability database. Third, run another vulnerability scan and review the report findings. Finally, review your upcoming scheduled scan jobs, verify the schedule details, and forward the schedule to your help desk so that it gets added to the IT maintenance calendar.

- *Using policies to take different actions with certain events* (e.g., bypass the SIEM function and go straight to logger) or to suppress entirely (e.g., you don't care about alerts that identify the use of Dropbox on employee's PCs).

- *Limiting the data a HIDS agent collects,* changing the verbosity of how an asset logs, or disabling services on a device to increase performance and/or throughput.

- *Completely changing the USM architecture to improve performance or segregate data* (such as breaking out an All-in-One appliance into its separate components –Server, Sensor and Logger).

ORIENT

Evaluate what is going on in the cyber threat landscape and inside your company. Make logical connections and apply real-time context to focus on priority events.

All of the information you've collected during the observation phase is essential for detecting a security event that requires your investigation. But information alone, without any context, is not sufficient for closed-loop incident response.

That's where the Orient phase comes in.

Contextual information is essential for orientation. All of the data in the world is useless without having the necessary context to understand the significance of that data. For example, a system outage in your data centre could either be an innocuous event (unexpected power failure) or something more serious (denial of service attack). Without the necessary context to orient you – for example, an email announcement from your ISP about the outage – you can't implement an effective response.

Your incident response goals during the Orient phase include:

- Determining the scope and impact of attack based on the latest threat intelligence;

- Reviewing the event in the context of other activity on the network to establish a timeline; and

- Investigating the source of the attack to determine attribution (if possible) and any additional intelligence that can assist decision-making.

Determine scope and impact of attack

Based on the latest threat intelligence, AlienVault Labs and AlienVault Open Threat Exchange (OTX) work together to monitor and analyse the latest attacker tools and tactics, and then convert this intelligence into automated actions (e.g. correlated rules, alarms, and tickets) within AlienVault USM so that you can effectively respond. These tools enable you to quickly determine which assets are affected and the severity of the activity or attack.

A specific example. In your AlienVault USM demo environment, you can see an alarm for an Exploitation and Installation event. On investigating further, you see that this involves an asset that's running a vulnerable version of Java. And it may not be the only asset on the network that's vulnerable. With AlienVault USM, you quickly review all events across all your assets to see what other systems have this type of activity and vulnerable configuration. In addition, you've automatically created an Asset Group based on these characteristics so that you can remediate all of these vulnerabilities as a group, and can continue to monitor them to validate these fixes. This "dynamic watchlist" enables you to have the essential context for an effective closed-loop incident response.

Review event in the context of other activity on the network to establish a timeline

AlienVault USM provides a unified timeline for all events to easily make connections between disparate but related events.

By viewing all events across a visual timeline, you can easily scan all of the security events and activity across your network – without having to consult multiple consoles, apps, or databases.

The simplified data visualisation approach makes it easy to make quick conclusions about which events require further investigation. In order to provide enough context yet not overwhelm your users, who are already overworked and under-appreciated, AlienVault chose to use a simplified design for USM's event timeline. The bigger the circle, the more types of events that have occurred within that category, and within that time frame.

Investigate source of attack to determine attribution (if possible) and any additional intelligence that can assist decision-making

According to cyber security expert Bruce Schneier, strong attribution can lead to deterrence. It can also provide the essential context to help detect and prevent future attacks and attackers that may share those same motivations, tools and techniques. The tight integration between AlienVault OTX and AlienVault USM enables our customers to use this intelligence for more reliable incident response.

The first two stages in the OODA loop – Observe and Orient – are all about security monitoring essentials. By gathering as much data as possible and then placing it in the context of local and global risk you can make the best decision possible.

DECIDE

Based on observations and context, choose the best tactic for minimal damage and fastest recovery.

These first two phases benefit from using automated tools for data collection and analysis, but deciding what to do based on this intelligence unfortunately can't be outsourced to non-humans. At least not yet.

That said, AlienVault Labs, AlienVault USM and AlienVault OTX provide as much guidance as possible for the best possible decision and outcome.

The key incident response goals for the Decide phase include the following:

- Determine the immediate next steps in responding to the incident.

- Review asset owner information and any relevant instructions associated with the asset.

- Document all remediation tactics planned for the affected assets.

Determine the immediate next steps
In responding to the incident, one of the biggest decisions that incident responders have is how to navigate the balancing act between the need to preserve evidence vs. the need to recover quickly.

This decision is best handled well in advance of your first incident. In fact, the standard operating procedure about handling incidents should come directly from senior management and the board of directors, with guidance from your legal team. Whether or not to preserve evidence vs. simply recover is not an easy decision to make, but one that you'll need to work out as soon as possible.

And please note, which way to go will often vary based on the industry you're in, the governing local law and state laws, the type of data in question, the method by which it was obtained, and whether or not this was an inside job vs. an outside one. As you can see, this is not a decision to take lightly, and AlienVault urge you to ask for guidance on this question. Intelligence and analysis on appropriate next steps is written by AlienVault Labs security researchers and integrated into each of the alarms in AlienVault USM.

Review asset owner information and any relevant instructions associated with the asset
When you're an incident responder, the more you know about the assets on your

network, the better you'll be at investigating incidents that involve them. This is especially true of the servers in your environment.

It's often not clear who owns an asset, how it's configured, or what software is installed, despite checking a variety of management tools, spreadsheets, and other docs. With AlienVault USM, you can document and review who owns an asset and what to do and who to contact in the event of an incident, as well as rich data on the vulnerabilities that exist, the software that's installed and running, and any recent changes to critical files.

Document all remediation tactics planned for the affected assets

Once you've confirmed the impact and scope of the incident, you'll need to remediate as quickly as possible to contain the damage and recover. It's a good idea to document these remediation steps with information on the specific assets as well as what was done, by whom, and when. An audit trail like this is very helpful, especially since at this point you don't know what kind of questions you'll get from your boss or his/her boss in the future.

AlienVault USM enables you to document all remediation steps within its automated and integrated trouble ticketing system. In fact, every alarm can be converted into a trouble ticket with just a simple click from within the alarm details. Additionally, you can monitor, review, and share trouble ticket resolution statistics on the AlienVault USM dashboard. All of this contributes to effective decision-making and process improvement.

ACT

Remediate and recover by improving incident response procedures based on lessons learned. By now, you've been walked through each of the first three phases of an effective incident response plan. You've been shown how AlienVault USM, AlienVault Labs, and AlienVault OTX provide the foundation you need to OBSERVE, ORIENT, and DECIDE how to respond to incidents. Now it's time to ACT.

But first… In the previous section, we talked about the need to decide whether your IR team should focus on preserving evidence (in order to prosecute a data breach) vs. recovering quickly (and potentially losing transient forensic artefacts). This important decision is far beyond the scope of this chapter. If you're interested in preserving data for further investigation, SIFT (SANS Investigative Forensics Toolkit) is a collection of various open source tools that can assist you in performing forensics analysis tasks also available from AlienVault.

In the meantime, this chapter has focused on recovery and remediation, as well as the specific ways that AlienVault helps you achieve these essential incident response goals within the **ACT** phase to:

- Quickly implement remediation on all affected assets and verify that remediation has been implemented properly;

- Review and update security awareness training programmes or security policies as appropriate; and

- Review (and potentially reconfigure) security monitoring controls based on lessons learned from the incident.

Quickly implement remediation
It's difficult to cover all of the possible remediation activities that you may need to implement, since it will largely depend on the specific threat, impact, targeted assets, and scope. That said, chances are that this will likely include activities such as:

- Patching systems (OSs, applications, firmware, etc.);

- Removing unnecessary or unauthorised software;

- Reconfiguring system files (e.g. removing DLLs, registry settings, etc.);

- Applying new ACLs on routers or adding firewall rules;

- Enabling or installing personal firewalls;

- Revoking access privileges;

- Resetting passwords;

- Terminating unused or unnecessary accounts;

    ... and more.

AlienVault USM helps you verify that remediation has been implemented properly in a variety of ways. First, its Vulnerability Assessment can be used to scan remediated hosts immediately after they've been patched, to verify fixes have worked, and haven't introduced additional risks. Additionally, the Asset Inventory capability captures and collects all asset data including installed and running software as well as open ports and services. These two capabilities combined help you confirm – at a glance – if a patch has been applied or a personal firewall installed or enabled.

Review and update security awareness training programs or security policies as appropriate

Every security incident investigation provides you with the opportunity to assess how well your security program is working (in terms of both security awareness and security policies and procedures). The more vigilant your users can be about cyber security, the more likely that the risk of incidents will decrease (in terms of frequency as well as impact).

A good first step is establishing effective user activity monitoring, so that you get a baseline for expected user behaviour. AlienVault USM provides detailed user activity reporting across all the assets in your environment so that you can verify that security policies are being followed, and any violations are documented and investigated. In addition, you can set up AlienVault USM to run reports at regularly scheduled intervals (the screenshot below captures just a few of the many reporting options for monitoring user activity).

Review (and potentially reconfigure) security monitoring controls based on lessons learned from the incident

Once you've completed and verified all necessary remediation steps (and this goes for patching systems as well as tweaking security policies), it's now time to do a critical analysis of the entire incident for essential lessons learned. Ask yourself and your team:

- What went well?

- What did we miss?

- What could we have done better?

During this analysis, you may discover the need to increase monitoring of certain assets or asset groups. With AlienVault USM, you can enable host-based IDS on specific assets and asset groups to monitor system performance as well as changes to critical system files.

Additionally, you may decide to do weekly vs. monthly vulnerability scans. AlienVault USM allows you to schedule vulnerability scans at any frequency, and offers a lot of options for how to execute these scans.

This chapter is an edited version the more detailed AlienVault White Paper entitled "AlienVault Incident Response Toolkit" which offers a clear account of cyber security good practice appropriate for most businesses.

Part Five

Cautionary Tales from the Frontline

5.1 THE POWER OF STORYTELLING

Nick Wilding, General Manager, Cyber Resilience, AXELOS

Storytelling, one of the oldest human practices, is one of the most powerful tools we have to combat the unprecedented threats we face, both individually and as part of our organisations, while, paradoxically, also being one of the most neglected. Dry 'tick-box' annual compliance training, with a 'one size fits all' approach, is still the typical approach yet this has demonstrably failed to embed the long-term behavioural changes required to operate securely, effectively and responsibly in the digital age. Storytelling can and should be an integral part of an effective enterprise-wide response to the cyber risks we face. Our emotional connection to these challenges, through stories, can be as powerful as technology in building the organisational, behavioural and cultural changes required to better protect our most precious information and systems. The chapters that follow are cautionary tales based on four real life incidents which could have happened to almost any unprotected company.

THE WHALE IN THE ROOM

In the first edition of *Managing Cybersecurity Risk* we cited the case of Jim Baines, CEO of Baines Packaging, who never knew he was a 'whale'[1] until he did something careless. Something he admits now was 'stupid' — he opened an attachment sent by someone he hardly knew, but who seemed credible. That casual error almost ruined his business, and destroyed his reputation and life.

Are you hooked? You should be. It's a story we're all familiar with. Any one of us

---

1. Whaling, in hacking terminology, is a malicious and fraudulent attack directed against a high-value individual, typically a C-level executive — the 'whale'. The attacks often employ spear-phishing email, lent credibility by socially engineering the target.

could have done what Jim did, found ourselves in his position — at the nexus of a crisis the outcome of which is maddeningly uncertain. If we're drawn to him, to his story, and the reasons why he fell into the trap set by hackers, it's perhaps because we don't want to look, but find it difficult to look away. That's the power of a good story. I believe it can, and should, be used to help us fight cybercrime and boost our resilience to attacks. In fact, it's one of the most efficient and effective ways of doing so. Why? Because telling stories is fundamental to our humanity.

Stories help us make sense of the world, to better understand its threats and opportunities, so we can mitigate the former and recognise and harness the latter. Simply put, our imaginations are what drive us. All the technical knowledge in the world, all the planning and analysis won't help if, fundamentally, you don't understand the essence of a threat or have an emotional investment (individually, collectively) in dealing with it.

That's what stories enable. They deal with human feeling, not jargon. They focus on broad but fundamental outcomes, and they drive action. That's the vital element: if you *feel* you need to act then you probably *will*. If you merely think about it, you might delay doing what's necessary to protect what you value until it's too late. Storytelling provides insight into the lessons learned by people like Jim (often through bitter experience) and highlights the ways stories, language and the adoption of a diverse range of learning tools and styles can assist organisations to develop a truly resilient, cyber-smart culture.

THE EFFECTIVENESS OF STORYTELLING

Storytelling is one of the oldest and purest forms of communication — and it works. Throughout humanity's existence, predating the invention of writing, we have made sense of our lives through the telling of stories.

Anthropologists and evolutionary biologists agree that it's a defining part of what makes us human. As one puts it:

'Like other species, humans can assimilate information through the rapid processing that specialised pattern recognition allows, but unlike other species, we also seek, shape and share information in an open- ended way.

Since pattern makes data swiftly intelligible, we actively pursue patterns, especially those that yield the richest inferences to our minds, in our most valuable information systems, the sense of sight and sound, and in our most crucial domain, social life.'[2]

Stories are social. When we share them with others, they invoke patterns of data that reveal lessons and survival strategies. We build on them in our minds by repeating

---

2. Boyd, B. (2009), On the Origin of Species, Harvard, Belknap.

them and embellishing them. Very soon they spread, warn and instruct. It's how bands of hunter-gatherers managed to survive in hostile environments. It's how we can survive in a world rife with cyber threats.

It also trumps the highly technical, jargon- heavy world of cybersecurity. A compelling story can resonate with audiences where dry reports fail to connect. As a *Harvard Business Review* article highlighted in 2014:

'A story will go where statistics, data and quantitative analysis are denied admission: our hearts. Data can persuade people, but it doesn't inspire them to act; to do that, you need to wrap your vision in a story that fires the imagination and stirs the soul.'[3]

As I have already stressed, stories spark emotions, and they help people to remember information.

REMEMBERING INFORMATION IN THE INFORMATION AGE

Over 100 years ago Hermann Ebbinghaus, an eminent German psychologist, pioneered the experimental study of memory. He is known for identifying the 'forgetting curve'. His results are widely accepted as a general theory for how we learn and retain information that remains valid today.

The bad news is that he found that 40 per cent of information presented as learning is forgotten in the first 20 minutes, more than half of all information is forgotten after one hour, and only a fifth of all information is remembered after one day. The good news is that there are strategies that can be used to improve memory retention. There are two primary factors:

- **Repetition**: the more frequently we repeat something, or provide complementary reminders, the more likely it is to stick. For cyber awareness learning, this means effectiveness is directly correlated to regular, ongoing updates, refreshers and reminders, which use varied techniques like animations, games, lunch and learn sessions, competitions and so forth.

- **Quality of meaning**: long-term retention and adoption is also dependent on the relevant, meaningful connections you can make between the new information and the things you already know. This is where stories and narrative are vital in making learning relevant and engaging, weaving cyber awareness into everything we do at home, in the workplace and on the move.

---

3. GOV.UK, 'Cyber Governance Health Check 2015/16', available at https://www.gov.uk/ government/ publications/cyber-governance-health- check-201516 (accessed 26th July, 2017).

LEADERSHIP BY EXAMPLE – THE BOARDROOM CHALLENGE

The author Maya Angelou famously wrote: 'I've learned that people will forget what you said, people will forget what you did, but people will never forget how you made them feel.' And what's the best way to make people feel? By telling a compelling story.

We know that effective cyber resilience requires clear leadership and informed insight from the top. We have seen that 90 per cent of successful cyber attacks succeed because of human error — and that includes the people who sit in the boardroom. So, stories can help our leaders not just understand that they have a problem but to *feel* that they have a key role to play in protecting their firm's most precious and valuable information.

At this stage, it may be instructive to look at sectors and industries that have traditionally been considered high risk and how they have developed, over decades, an enterprise-wide safety and security-conscious mindset and culture. For example, the nuclear industry places high value on what it calls the 'Implementation of Good Human Behavioural Performance'. The Essential Guide to the industry states:

'The collective behaviours of individuals in an organisation determine the level of safety and performance achieved. Their performance is influenced by diverse factors related to the management style, work environment and the demands of the task as well as their own individual capabilities. At high-performing sites, individuals at all levels take responsibility for their behaviours and are committed to improving themselves, executing the task correctly and improving their work environment. In general, individuals exhibit the following behaviours:

- Communicate to create a shared understanding of good practice within their peer groups.

- Anticipate error-likely situations.

- Improve personal capabilities.

- Report near-miss events together with explanation of the causes.

- Implement techniques for improving Human Performance of the organisation.'[4]

In the digital age, all industries and sectors that extensively utilise information technologies should consider themselves 'high risk'. Everyone in an organisation,

---

4. http://namrc.co.uk/wp-content/uploads/2013/03/ NIA-essential-guide-2.pdf (accessed 4 August, 2017).

from top to bottom, needs to understand those risks and have the confidence and responsibility to make the right decision at the right time. Equally, if — and, almost inevitably, when — mistakes are made, these should be seen as opportunities to learn rather than triggers for disciplinary action. Learning and storytelling must play a crucial role in this.

A new, more holistic approach is required: one where information security and cyber awareness learning is conceived of as a continuous, ongoing and sustainable campaign. Just as our technical security controls must constantly evolve and adapt to combat changing cyber threats and vulnerabilities, so we need to ensure all our people maintain their awareness learning and are provided with appropriate practical guidance on a continuing basis that fits the needs and requirements of the organisation. To achieve this, we need to provide a range of learning techniques that truly engage all our people, helping to embed and sustain the resilient behaviours required to effect the systemic and cultural change we wish to see.

GUIDING PRINCIPLES

There are some simple guiding principles to consider when assessing whether your cyber awareness learning campaign is and remains effective and engaging:

Leadership: Lead by example — getting the buy-in and involvement of those at the top can highlight the positive benefits of resilient behaviours, assist in rewarding and inspiring all staff, and illustrate how seriously your organisation is committed to protecting its most sensitive information and assets. Jim Baines now believes that he should have taken a more proactive role in thinking and talking about cybersecurity instead of leaving it to his technical team. They, inevitably, were focused on what seemed like more urgent operational matters. 'It's up to a company's leaders to get the issue up the agenda', he says. 'And lead by example — that is, don't be careless with email and laptops and flash drives! Follow your own rules.'

Reinforce the message: Memories are fragile, so always plan to refresh and evolve the learning content and delivery techniques with your staff on a regular basis. Combining formats with offline activities such as live events, competitions, surveys and team learning sessions can help sustain and instil the understanding and importance of new behaviours.

Accommodate different learning styles: People learn differently, so develop your campaign around a lively mix of online formats — games, animation, simulations and videos — to enable people to choose their preferred learning style but which ultimately deliver the same learning outcomes. Exploiting the latest developments in game play, for example, will immerse the learner in the problem and help to provide simple, pragmatic advice for how to recognise and 'beat' an attack.

Use every means at your disposal: Always stay agile, always adapt, fine tune, pilot new techniques and react quickly to the latest attack stories and how they affect your people. Also consider identifying team 'champions' and 'mentors' who you can involve in the design, not just in the learning. This has been seen to help build a powerful learning culture from the bottom up, not just from the top down.

Storytelling: As we have discussed, people remember stories more readily than dry facts. Critically, ensure you fix a message in your learners' minds by appealing to their hearts. Great campaigns have great stories to tell. The cyberattack statistics are available for all to see and yet organisations remain highly vulnerable to even the simplest phishing emails. Talk about business impacts, talk about personal and professional consequences. Use role play and realistic scenarios to bring the message home, not (just) tech jargon and statistics.

The merits of this approach were forcefully espoused by Angela Sasse, Professor of Human-Centred Technology at UCL and Director of the UK Research Institute in Science of Cyber Security (RISCS), at the European Information Security Summit in February 2017. She said that engagement is the key to a truly effective awareness training programme. To achieve it:

'You need to really work with your people and embark on having ongoing conversations with them about what the threats are out there. That's what we want to change — we want people to talk about security, discuss the risks, but help each other out. The more people talk about security to each other, the better things will become.'[5]

CONCLUSION: MEET JIM BAINES

There are a lot of 'Jims' out there. But, at this stage I must reveal that the much quoted Jim is not a real person. He is, in fact, a fictional character. He comes to life in a novel published as a part-work, *Whaling for Beginners*. The story is populated by a lively cast of characters and the narrative unfolds swiftly from multiple points of view, allowing the reader to understand and identify with the motives of all those directly involved — from the hacker to the executives affected by the hack. It's an approach that has proved remarkably effective.

As Richard Knowlton, Chairman of Richard Knowlton Associates and former Vodafone Group Director of Corporate Security, has commented:

'I hate to think how many worthy presentations I've sat through on cyber risk management in the boardroom, so my first reaction on reading Whaling for Beginners

---

5. Samarati, M. (March 2017), 'Switch to engaging staff awareness training', available at https://www.itgovernance.co.uk/blog/switch-to-engaging-staff-awareness-training/ (accessed 26th July, 2017).

was, "At last!" Instead of a technical tract heavy on acronyms and terms of art, here's a very realistic human story … an essential lesson for boards, so often bedazzled by the apparently impenetrable specialist technical nature of cyber. Directors need to understand that while they will need some specialist advice (just as they do over legal or tax matters, for example), they need to see cyber risk as an integral part of their general enterprise risk management process.'

Stories make us human. They have helped us build civilisations. They give us the understanding and ambition we need to protect our achievements. I've been talking about Jim Baines, quoting his (fictional) words, to a wide range of audiences. They instantly understand his pain, and his need to fight back. When they discover that he isn't real it doesn't change anything. Why? Because his story has engaged their emotions, their sense of self, reputation and ambition. It's what the best stories do. We identify with strong characters, from Ulysses to Hamlet, Sherlock Holmes to George Smiley. It's entertainment but it's also instruction. We learn about strategy and danger and opportunity and achievement through stories. That's why we can't help but engage with them in all their myriad forms.

The hackers tell stories about us. Their narratives say we're too slow, flawed and myopic to see through their wiles, and too staid to keep up with their ingenious tricks. We're not. We can resist and fight back. But only if we understand what's really at stake — human livelihoods and reputations — and change our ways to protect them. Jim's story is already doing that. It's being read by many executives. It's changing attitudes and energising positive action. That's why I believe we need to tell more stories. *Imagine if we did* — we might just steal a march on the hackers and make their lives much, much harder!

If you would like to find out more, you can contact Nick Wilding at nick.wilding@axelos.com

5.2 HOW TO AVOID THAT 'I TOLD YOU SO' MOMENT

A real life story from AXELOS RESILIA

This account of a cyber breach is a true story, but details have been changed to protect both the organisation and the participants.

HOW TO AVOID THAT 'I TOLD YOU SO' MOMENT

Making precise predictions about the future at board meetings is always a dangerous game. But, when I told my colleagues on the board of a large multinational retailer that the organisation would be hacked, and probably already had been hacked, they looked at me with a mixture of disbelief, disdain and amusement.

The company had just been through a complex merger with an Asian competitor, and our agenda was full of issues relating to streamlining our international operations and leveraging the benefits of the alliance to our complex supply-chain. Cybersecurity was not a priority. The share price was fluctuating, and our brand needed to be bolstered at a time of uncertainty. The threat from some teen hacker in his bedroom, or even an organised crime group seemed remote and ephemeral. One of my colleagues said, "We spent a fortune on IT, how the hell could anyone get through all that money?!"

As Chief Security Officer, I'd spent most of my time trying to educate my colleagues that security was not just a technical issue. It was about people. Our people. The people working for our suppliers. And all the people who enter our store; namely, our customers. But the message had fallen on stubbornly deaf ears. That hadn't stopped me from taking the role of the board's cybersecurity Cassandra. I wrote a paper which tried to outline the weaknesses across our organisation, especially after the merger. I'll quote from it:

'There are few certainties in 21st century business, but one of them is that there will be a cyber breach of some kind, somewhere. I can guarantee that we will be hacked. That is, if we haven't already suffered some kind of incursion which we haven't even detected yet. For me the weakest point in our defences is our stores. A recent audit committee report pointed out that security procedures amongst staff are lax – especially when it comes to passwords used to access our customer database where much of our sensitive information (credit cards, names and addresses, and personal details) resides. Morale in the stores is lower than it should be and this is due to lack of investment in staff training, especially in terms of security.'

The report was circulated, minuted, discussed briefly, and attracted assurances of action – once the merger had been completed and the dust had settled out in the marketplace. Simply, the board kicked the issue into the long grass and focused on numbers: the cost of the merger, the savings it would deliver, and the effect on the share price. Security was a secondary – technical – issue that we'd get to later.

But events always conspire to undermine expectations. And in our case, the event stemmed from exactly the source I'd highlighted in my paper: a disaffected employee in one of our stores.

It was an 'I told you so' moment which I grasped eagerly. Not to gloat over my prescience, but to ensure that my colleagues learned from the lesson. Cybersecurity is NOT simply a technical issue, it's fundamentally also a people issue.

This is what happened.

One Sunday morning, about three months after the merger had hit the headlines and our stores had been re-branded with some fanfare (i.e. a big advertising spend), a headline appeared on the front of a leading paper:

WANT TO HACK OUR CUSTOMERS' CREDIT CARD DETAILS? SURE, STEP RIGHT IN!

The first paragraph was devastating: it related how the journalist had been given the password to our database and had then entered our system, found her own personal records (credit card number, address, mother's maiden name, online password, purchase history etc.), and downloaded them. It got worse: her partner happened to be a midranking government official in the diplomatic service, and his details were also readily available. She downloaded them too.

The article pointed out that not only were ordinary customers' details freely available, but that prominent persons, from government to culture to sports, could be found via our insecure database. The threat to our brand – and of course the danger of regulatory repercussions – was immense. That one article was bound to knock a sizeable chunk of value from our share price when trading opened on the Monday. I knew that press reception of the merger had been a little sceptical to begin with, but this 'breach' would fuel the fire. Those who thought that the business strategy behind the merger was unsound, would now have ammunition to further undermine confidence. And our negligence had given them that ammunition. To mix metaphors; it was an own goal.

I had to act quickly.

> 'The threat to our brand – and of course the danger of regulatory repercussions – was immense.'

I contacted my fellow board members and got them on a conference call. One of them was gracious enough to mention my paper. Suddenly, the warnings I'd included made sense. But it was too late to go back. We had to deal with the fallout and get ahead of the story. For me, that meant admitting that there were problems and we had a plan in place to address the problem: low employee morale and training in our stores.

I could claim that we did because I'd written that paper. It was 'spin' but necessary 'spin'.

The journalist's source was the assistant manager of a store in a small town located in a territory that we knew needed more investment. He'd been passed over for promotion, and angry about the merger and subsequent changes to his benefits and employment contract. That's why he decided to talk to the press. But, he had something to talk about: our lax security. In his store, everyone used the same password to access customer details. Even temporary staff were given the password and told to search our records. The password was never changed. It was very simple and easy to crack – though, of course, no one needed to waste time cracking it because it was written down for all to see by the till!

> 'In his store, everyone used the same password to access customer details.'

These issues could've been easily addressed. It didn't take a lot of money – or technology – to protect our database through each of our stores: all we had to do was put a policy in place that restricted access to sensitive data to employees with specific authorised roles, mandated tough passwords that had to be changed on a strict rota, and ensure good security practice within the store. But we hadn't done that.

When I'd pressed for investment in training and the adoption of better systems and processes, I was told that budgets were under pressure due to the merger. That the priority was to push for increased revenues and profits so that the market would respond well to the merger. Security just was not a priority. As I said at the start, no one anticipated a breach might happen, even though I'd highlighted the conditions that were increasing the risk of one occurring many times before.

> 'We quickly brought in a specialist training company to plan a company-wide programme to upgrade staff knowledge of security'

Once the story broke, the share price tumbled, and the brand took a hit. With the logic behind the merger coming into question from wider sources (including governments), the board were eager to ask me what needed to be done and how much they should spend on it.

It wasn't too late, luckily.

The fact that the source of the story was one of our own employees meant that it was possible that the passwords hadn't been used by hackers. The assistant manager's decision to talk pre-empted any wider breach. However, of course, we couldn't be sure, so we went into lockdown. Changed all the passwords. Restricted access. Reviewed our security procedures and trawled through all the areas where malicious code might be lingering, either leaking data or about to. We didn't find anything. That was down to luck. I can't put it down to anything other than luck. It certainly wasn't by design.

We quickly brought in a specialist training company to plan a companywide programme to upgrade staff knowledge of security and how to protect data. But, I made sure that the emphasis was on improving skills and raising morale. If morale is high, then you're in a much better position to avoid an 'insider' threat: the possibility that an employee with privileged access goes to the dark side, or, more commonly, just gets complacent.

The only bad luck was that the journalist that our employee went to happened to be a customer of ours. And that bad luck was doubled by the fact that their partner was not only a customer too, but also a government official. But that's the way things can go: bad luck compounds bad practice. The only thing you're in control of is the way you set up your business and the good practice you instil in your people at all levels of the organisation.

And it's not just at store level, it's at board level too that good practice counts. There, in the supposedly rarefied atmosphere where great strategic decisions are made, losing sight of the simple truth that security matters just as much as the share price or quarterly revenue figures is vital. Those revenues will only be as strong as your brand, and its reputation is founded not just on customer service but also confidence in your ability to manage and protect sensitive data. Not just customer data, but intellectual property, and supply chain logistics too. If any, or all, are hacked then they can be fatally undermined in practice as well as theory.

'Don't give someone the chance to tell you that they told you so.'

Six months after we dealt with the incident, I decided to move on. I relinquished my seat on the board as Chief Security Officer and began a new life as a consultant. I find that my experience of a breach that could have had such serious repercussions has stood me in good stead. Now, my exhortations to take security seriously and focus on people more than technology are listened to.

I took some satisfaction from my valedictory speech to my colleagues on the day I left: I took the courage to say, 'I told you so'. And they took it in good spirits. They told me I was right. Now that doesn't happen too often in business, let alone life in general.

Don't give someone the chance to tell you that they told you so.

If you would like to find out more, you can contact Nick Wilding at nick.wilding@axelos.com

5.3 A CUCKOO IN THE NEST?

A real life story from AXELOS RESILIA

This account of a cyber-breach is a true story, but details have been changed to protect both the organisation and the participants.

A CUCKOO IN THE NEST?

"Is this normal?" That's not a subject heading a Chief Security Officer likes to see in their inbox of a morning. It usually means a problem has been discovered that has, most probably, been going on for a while. With a sense of distinct trepidation, I opened the email from one of my security team. It read:

'Helen in logistics seems to be doing a lot of overtime suddenly. She's pulled two all-nighters in a week. Is that normal for her? She's logging on at 10pm through to 6am (Tuesday / Wednesday) – and 4am through 8am on Thursday. Wasn't that the software refresh? She's not involved in that, is she? Should I investigate?'

My first instinct was to run down to the department and scream at the team, but I resisted. It's not good management practice. And, maybe Helen (whom I knew only vaguely) needed the overtime for a specific reason – perhaps she was saving for a holiday, or a deposit for a flat. I wondered why the manager who had contacted me hadn't bothered to check with her before emailing me. I had been arguing for more funds to refresh the security training of my team, and the email stiffened my resolve to argue more forcibly at the next board meeting.

But, very quickly, my thoughts turned to the distinct possibility that 'Helen' wasn't Helen, but someone using her login details to – well, do nefarious things (to put it mildly). I picked up the phone to the Head of Logistics. Asked her to get Helen to give me a call immediately. And within a minute she was on the phone.

"This is a simple question, and don't worry about its implications," I said.

"That's making me nervous, sorry." She was right. It wasn't a good opening.

"OK, forgive me, but we might have a problem."

"With me?"

"No, your login details."

"Oh."

"Have you been working through the night on something?"

She laughed. "No! With my 18-month-old son at home, it's a miracle I work through the day!"

"OK, I see. Have you shared your login credentials with anyone?"

"No." There was doubt in her voice.

"No?"

"Umm... a while back... I mean, a month or so ago, Frank needed them urgently to... you know... get into the system to do something."

"Frank?"

"Yeah, from XWare."

I immediately realised what was happening. I thanked Helen for her honesty. Reminded her that she should not share any login credentials with anyone, for whatever reason, whoever they were, and told her that I'd get hold of Frank.

Who was Frank exactly?

He worked for a contractor organization that was overseeing a transformation of our logistics. We'd decided to digitalise our entire operation. It was part of the transformation the board had ordered to help us deflect nimble start-ups which were threatening to impinge on our market share in transport business.

We'd set a tight deadline. Our consultants had scared the board into action with doom-laden stories of how we could be the Kodak of the transport industry: a tired, bloated behemoth unable to muster the agility needed to ward off competitors who had no legacy systems or costs to slow them down.

That deadline was so tight, the contractor's staff were under pressure to deliver. I was uneasy about that from the start: rushing something always leads to problems, both technical and, more importantly, in terms of security. By rushing into the future to defend ourselves, we were lowering our guard to criminals after our current riches.

Frank was the symbol of that danger now, in my mind, at least. I had to track what he'd been doing, and talk to him directly. I called around the company – he wasn't due back into the office until lunchtime.

My team quarantined all Helen's work. We started to trace what Frank had been doing under her name during those long night-time sessions. For a few hours, we played detective, and discovered that he had been working to get the new software aligned to complex logistics systems. The work was normal. He had not accessed databases, only linked them together in line with the rollout plan.

By around 11.30am that day I could breathe a sigh of relief. Frank was not a hacker. He wasn't working for hackers. He seemed benign, a software engineer under pressure from his managers to get the work done on time. But that didn't excuse the way he'd gone about his work.

Helen was at fault for sharing her credentials with him – to help him out, admittedly – but it was still against best practice. She needed better training. In fact, the whole team needed it.

They didn't just need training in how to create good passwords and keep them private, they also needed to be shown how to resist the temptation to let contractors become part of 'the team.'

If Frank had been a 'bad actor', he'd have bided his time until he was well-known to everyone; trusted, great company, the kind of guy you asked out for drinks on a Friday night after work... and then he'd wheedle his way into passwords and codes and, finally, steal stuff.

But this Frank wasn't doing that. Luckily for us. The principle is, though, that contractors may not be who they purport to be. So, all credentials must be kept safe, and contractors should only be granted rights of access which are directly pertinent to the specific work that they are doing. No more, no less. And there needs to be a dual-key held by an employee for anything that's remotely sensitive to the health and security of the business.

I had to take some blame for the situation. In the rush towards 'digital transformation' we'd got sloppy with security. We'd become too friendly with the contractors. They'd become 'friends' – and 90% of the time that's not going to hurt you. But, as all users of digital media will know, there's always a small chance that that an apparently friendly message isn't really from a friend. He or she may be a hacker.

The lesson is simple: be friendly with your clients, contractors and customers but always keep your secrets in the family. Monitor who's doing what and when, and look for unusual patterns – such as someone like Helen working all night when she's never done it before – and respond quickly. Investigate, be suspicious, never take someone for granted, especially an outsider. Beware a cuckoo in the nest.

'She needed better training. In fact, the whole team needed it.'

**If you would like to find out more, you can contact Nick Wilding at
nick.wilding@axelos.com**

5.4 THE TROUBLE WITH CONTRACTORS

A real life story from AXELOS RESILIA

This account of a cyber-breach is a true story, but details have been changed to protect both the organisation and the participants.

THE TROUBLE WITH CONTRACTORS

In my experience as a Chief Security Officer, I've come across more problems with people than technology. Hardware and software may or may not work properly, but they are easy to track and modify. People are different. People are the most vulnerable element within your organisation when it comes to security.

Not just your salaried employees, but your contractors too. In fact, contractors can be even more problematic because it's easy to forget that they're actually there! I work on the principle that if a contractor is doing a job for longer than a couple of years, then you should probably be employing someone (or a team) to do it in-house. By doing that you will have more control, not just over what they're doing and how they're doing it, but also over their security practices.

And security is the point. How many times have you read a story about a so-called 'third party' cyber attack in which hackers have, for instance, gained access to a large company's intellectual property via the software that runs the air-conditioning, or even (and this is true) through a routinely used fast-food outlet?

It happens all too often. And it's easy to stop.

I learned about this danger the hard way. A few years ago, I was happily holidaying in a balmy climate far from the office when I received an urgent call. I knew it was urgent because my secretary was under strict instructions to contact me only in the event of an emergency. So, when her name appeared on the screen of my phone, I knew my holiday was about to be ruined.

"Someone is syphoning off data and sending it God knows where," was the way she put it. Immediately, the image of liquid ones and zeroes flowing out of the company and into a hooded hacker's oil can sprang to mind. Naturally, I knew it wasn't that simple. I got on the phone to my colleagues back at head office and began to unravel the situation.

What was clear was that large quantities of data were being packaged up and encrypted and then sent out of the company using a supposedly secure access point. Whoever was doing it knew the passwords and had administrative rights. It was an inside job. I assumed it was a disaffected employee – or, perhaps, one who had been paid generously to steal the data.

It didn't take long to find the access point and, with a modicum of sleuthing, the person responsible. It wasn't an employee, but a contractor. An individual who had been working within our company – under the auspices of a contractor assigned a range of tasks a full five years before – but who was not directly employed by us.

We didn't alert him to what we knew straight away. We called the police and they advised that we track his movements and actions to see where the data was going. I should explain that we were operating within the healthcare sector, and it was important to understand whether any of our manufacturing operations were being compromised, or IP secrets sold to competitors or even what are known as 'state actors'.

The 'hacker' – though that's a misnomer as he was granted full access by us and didn't have to do any actual hacking – was known to our staff as a loner. He was someone who did a lot of overtime, worked weekends and late nights, seemed to have little social life, and made no effort to forge friendships despite his long service within our organisation.

That alone should have raised alarm bells. I realised that we had never made the effort to get to know the people the contractor had employed. We just assumed they'd send the right people. We were focused on the outcomes, not the personnel or the methods.

'Contractors can be even more problematic because it's easy to forget that they're actually there!'

That turned out to be our first mistake.

Our second was to assume that the individual was respectful of the integrity of the contractor for whom they worked, that they would follow the practices and procedures as laid down in the contract that we, as a board, had signed with their board. It can all seem so cosy at the top; convivial contractual discussions over lunch, and a casual signing of papers with expectations that everyone involved is benefitting. But it behoves any C-level office, especially those with responsibility for security, to stand on the frontline and meet the people doing the actual work. Because that's where you're vulnerable.

We didn't do that. This individual managed to gain the confidence of our people, and was able to work with minimal oversight. He took the opportunity to sell our data to someone else.

Eventually, we cut off his access and the police arrested him. He claimed that he was doing it as an 'exercise' to prove that our systems were vulnerable and that he was about to inform us of that fact with 'evidence'. That is, the fact he'd been able to package up data and move it out beyond our firewalls.

> 'This individual managed to gain the confidence of our people, and was able to work with minimal oversight.'

It was a story of course but it was useful. For that, I'm grateful. It reinforced some important lessons. We should:

- Monitor all contractors constantly

- Try to keep roles that can directly impact cybersecurity in-house and under our complete control

- Always get to know both staff and contractors so that we can identify any signs of waywardness or disaffection. This has to be done sensitively, of course.

And, if contractors do need privileged access, there should be a 'dual key' held by an in-house member of the management team (preferably within the IT security department) so that no contractor can wander at will through our databases without us knowing about it.

If you would like to find out more, you can contact Nick Wilding at nick.wilding@axelos.com

5.5 HACKED INTO A PARALLEL UNIVERSE

A real life story from AXELOS RESILIA

This account of a cyber breach is a true story, but details have been changed to protect both the organization and the participants.

HACKED INTO A PARALLEL UNIVERSE

I read a revealing interview with Dido Harding, the outgoing CEO of UK telecoms provider TalkTalk, where she mentioned that the very public and damaging breach her company suffered in late 2015 made her feel as if she was suddenly 'in a foreign land'. I knew how she felt. But for me, what happened felt less like being transported to a distant country – it was more akin to being phased into a parallel universe! On the surface everything looked the same, but I knew that it very definitely wasn't.

The moment I got that phone call, time seemed to both speed up and slow down. It was as if I'd become a character in a thriller by John Le Carré, by way of The Matrix. It was Easter Monday and I was at home doing the usual kinds of things I did on British bank holidays. I think I was planting bulbs for the summer when I heard the phone chirrup in the kitchen. It was my work phone ringtone and my first thought was that someone was calling about a workshop that was due to take place the next day. The on-screen details indicated that it was my boss calling. That threw me as I knew he was abroad, taking a long overdue break. Why would he be contacting me now?

I was Chief Security Officer for our company – a large, multi-market, global organization with a mix of production and retail operations. As such I bore responsibility for protecting the company from cyber-attacks but, although I was conscious that one might happen at any time, it didn't even occur to me that this might be about that. I know now how naïve that was.

"What are you doing tomorrow?" he asked. He sounded too calm. Normally, he spoke in terse sentences which some found too direct. I was used to that; in fact, I appreciated his straightforward approach. You always knew where you were with him. But this was different.

"We're doing the workshop," I said.

"Get someone else to do it. Come down to London and be in my office by ten. Can you do that?"

"Sure, but..."

"I can't tell you what it's about yet."

I hadn't had time to ask, but his statement stopped me arranging the words of a very obvious question in the right order. He hung up before I had the chance to ask it. Naturally, the rest of that Easter Monday was ruined. I imagined all kinds of fanciful scenarios, even ones where I, or someone in my team, was about to be fired. I slept fitfully and in the morning I took the early train and tried to work, but couldn't really concentrate on anything.

When I entered my boss's office I could see that he'd had as little sleep as I'd had. His usual confident demeanour had been undermined. It was evident something bad had happened – or was happening.

"I got a call yesterday... from..." He hesitated. He was clearly choosing words that he'd been told to use, but was uncomfortable with. "From an 'agency'."

"What kind of agency?"

"Let's just keep this... simple, shall we?" He was irritable and I decided to comply. Further questions would only prolong the tension. "It seems we've been breached."

"Breached?"

"They believe... we believe that there has been… 'activity' from two unrecognised IP addresses in our network. They want us to investigate them." He pushed a piece of paper toward me on which were printed two web addresses. The neat blue print belied the potential danger they represented to our organisation, our reputation... perhaps even our jobs.

"OK. And these are...?"

"Probably criminal... possibly even... state-sponsored."

"State-sponsored?"

My boss shook his head. The implication was clear: no further questions, just investigate.

"I've arranged an emergency restricted board meeting – I want you to come and explain what you know, but essentially all I want you to say is, 'I think we have a problem.' Don't be specific. Don't indulge in speculation. I don't want to panic them; just look into it and describe the situation as simply as you can."

I left the room in a dilemma. Should I tell the IT team what was happening? But no one had a clue what was happening! The unnamed 'agency' had just supplied two IP addresses, which may or may not be malicious. But they must be – or they wouldn't have supplied them. I knew I had to reveal some of what was happening to the IT team.

When I did, they were incredulous. It couldn't be possible. Our systems were sound. "It's fiction," the IT director told me. "Someone's been watching too many spy films."

What dawned on me during those first few hours was how unprepared we all were for an actual breach. We really believed that we were impregnable, that we'd done enough to secure our network and protect our sensitive data. Despite all the stories that regularly appeared in the news – commercial enterprises and government departments, large and small, compromised and customer data syphoned off into the Dark Web – the bottom line was, we were still complacent about the possibility of it happening to us.

And we'd also created a situation in which merely investigating a possible breach was hugely complex. We'd outsourced a lot of our IT to a third party and, as it turned out, we were relying too heavily on technology. In some ways, even though we turned over hundreds of millions of pounds annually, we were only as secure and every bit as vulnerable as the average domestic PC user!

> 'We'd outsourced a lot of our IT to a third party and, as it turned out, we were relying too heavily on technology.'

When I contacted the third party, they said it would take weeks to investigate, and that they would have to charge us extra fees to do the work. I was speechless. Surely, it was part of the original contract? Turned out it wasn't. Why? Because cyber security had not been seen as a priority at the time it was negotiated. There were no adequate service level agreements in place — the board had looked to save pennies, and as a result had stymied the organisation's ability to be agile in the face of a threat, and resilient if it turned out to be real.

I had no choice but to authorise a payment to the third party supplier and hope that the threat would mollify a board that seemed more concerned about improving profit margins (marginally) than protecting the very integrity of our organisation. The initial investigation – eased by the payment – took three days. And the conclusion? Yes, the IP addresses we'd been given had entered our system. But there was no indication as to who was behind them, or what they were doing. Nothing seemed to be amiss, except that a breach had occurred.

I had to face the board. So, I carefully framed my words in a way that was designed not to alarm them, just as my boss had asked me to, though, I believed that they needed to be alarmed, as this was, in truth, at least partly their fault.

"An unidentified adversary has managed to introduce malware onto the network for reasons unknown."

They were alarmed. In fact, they were shocked. They couldn't believe it. My boss had reviewed the words to try to ensure it seemed like a routine event in cyber security monitoring, but the board's lack of knowledge on the subject meant that their first instinct was to panic. What alarmed them the most was the fact that we hadn't discovered it ourselves, but an outside 'agency' had alerted us to it.

I was given complete ownership of the problem. I had to find out where the breach had occurred, what the malware was, and, most importantly, what it was doing. Were we about to suffer the same headlines as other similar organisations?

HACKERS STEAL MILLIONS OF PERSONAL DETAILS! YOUR PERSONAL INFORMATION IS BEING TRADED BY CRIMINALS!

That was what worried them most. Their reputations were on the line.

The third party supplier managed to create a detailed timeline of the breach and the activities of the malware. It had happened six months ago! And the malware had, as yet, not been activated. It was just sitting there, watching, listening – brooding. In some ways that felt worse than if there had already been a theft of data. What was it for? Who was behind it?

My colleague in the IT team wondered if it was waiting for a specific activity or message that contained a keyword. Maybe it was to do with a big negotiation that was going on with a large overseas supplier.

The contract, if it was signed, would be worth billions over the next decade. Perhaps some state agency was monitoring it? Why? To undermine it, maybe, or just to know the details ahead of its public announcement. No one could work it out.

So, how did the breach happen?

Hollywood movies have encouraged us to imagine intricate Mission Impossible style operations…men wearing balaclavas, with headsets, swinging through the dark on zip-wires... but it turned out to be nothing more than a mundane phishing email.

A senior finance manager had seen an email addressed to him which had as its subject line: 'Overdue invoice'. He opened it, clicked on a PDF of the invoice and saw that it was not for his department and that his name – which was a fairly common name, let's call him 'John Brown' – had been confused with a finance guy in operations. So, he forwarded the email.

The second John Brown was on holiday, so it just sat in his inbox. The first John Brown, though, had already fallen for the scam and, by opening the PDF, the malware was now in the system. It burrowed its way into a specific part of it, and sat there. We called 'John Brown 1' and spun him a story about upgrading his laptop, and he brought it in. We investigated the bogus email and then cleaned up the computer.

It was clear that both Browns were targeted solely to get into the system. We speculated that the hackers had merely chosen a series of very common British names and sent out hundreds, even thousands, of phishing emails hoping someone would take the bait. They got two bites. And, when the second John Brown got back from holiday, he clicked on the PDF too. Which was why there were now two unrecognized IP addresses in the system.

> 'It turned out to be nothing more than a mundane phishing email.'

We shared the information and the 'agency' suddenly became more talkative. They complimented our forensics, but asked us (very politely but firmly) not to block the malware. The board had to agree to that and they were sceptical: 'What do we get out of it?' they asked. I argued that it would help them to protect us and other companies and, besides, the malware had been there for six months already, a few more weeks would make no difference. And, of course, we were monitoring it now.

The board were very worried. They were concerned something would be lost or compromised and there'd a leak to the press. The sensitive negotiations on the big international contract were bound to be the reason for the breach. It could all fall through, the share price would plummet and the headlines would be toxic. Plus, the Information Commissioner would have to be informed and then... well, that was a real can of worms (the ICO recently handed down a record fine to TalkTalk for its perceived 'security failings').

I urged calm. One board member said he knew someone in the Government and he'd have a word. We told him not to; that we should just put probes in the system and watch. 'They' – whoever 'they' were – could keep on watching us, and we would watch them. The negotiations should continue, but with extra security measures and vigilance. And that's what we did.

I don't know how we did it, but we kept the whole thing quiet. There were no headlines. No leaks. And the malware snoozed. I made sure we worked out contingency plans to cover all eventualities. We did wargames. We beefed up our security. We brought the security function back in-house. But because we kept a tight 'circle of trust' (some board members didn't even know what was happening) we contained the potential for panic and damaging rumours spreadingany further.

All the while we monitored and probed, the 'agency' carried out its own investigations. They told us exactly nothing about what they were doing or who they were looking at, which kept us all on edge. But I was determined to use this episode to show the organisation just how important the whole issue was, that we should never have to go through this experience in the same way again. And then the 'agency' delivered its report. As suspected, it was a 'zero-day' attack. The malware was waiting for a key event relating to our negotiations with a foreign supplier. The 'agency' had all the information they needed and they ordered us to shut the malware down. Which we did, immediately.

> 'The malware was waiting for a key event relating to our negotiations with a foreign supplier.'

No further details were given to us. That was frustrating, but it was also understandable. The main benefit of the whole episode – apart from the fact that no data was stolen, and no embarrassing headlines undermined our reputation – was that it gave me the chance to start an intensive awareness learning programme across the organisation.

The fact that a senior manager had fallen for a phishing email made my point for me. It's people who count as much as systems. You can't rely solely on anti-virus, firewalls, software patches or ever more sophisticated access controls. Your people have to be educated, trained, and vigilant enough to resist falling for the simple, obvious scams as well.

Our organisation signed the deal. We're trading much more securely, and I can safely say that we're far more resilient. We've had a couple of incidents where a manager has gone to a fake 'watering hole' site (one designed to look like a legitimate site that is frequently visited by the target or targets) where there was been a potential for breach, but otherwise we've stayed secure.

> 'It's a hard reality that in the digital age no organisation can hope to be 100% secure from cyber-attacks'

Most importantly, our cyber security is in our own hands now. We own it, we run it. That's not always possible for organisations smaller than ours of course. Many smaller companies have no choice but to work with a third party for their IT security, but as our experience showed, if you do, it's important to be very clear about their contractual terms and their obligations in the event of a breach.

We have worked hard to create a culture in which cyber security is very high on every agenda, and regular reports are made to the board to keep the issue front-of-mind. Now, our board is keen to hear those reports and they take them extremely seriously. They know they had a near miss and they're determined not to have another one. And as for 'John Brown 1'? Well, we didn't even tell him what that PDF had started – but we did make sure he got the training he needed to be more alert in the future.

Now, looking back, I wonder about the different things I could have done, or the range of consequences that could have followed on from the breach. I try to imagine those parallel universes, the many worlds in which I had acted differently, or the malware had been activated with dire results. In some I was heroic, but in most, to be honest, chaos reigned and I ended up losing my job. Luckily, though, we took the right action. We got the right help and we opened our eyes to the threats.

I would urge everyone in a position of seniority and influence in their organisation to take stock of their existing cyber security measures, their understanding of the nature and whereabouts of their key information assets, the ongoing effectiveness of their all-staff awareness training programme (if indeed they have one!) and their relationships with their key suppliers if they don't wish to find themselves similarly transported to unfamiliar and hazardous terrains. It's a hard reality that in the digital age no organisation can hope to be 100% secure from cyber-attacks but with the right balance of technical controls, operational processes, and training programmes in place you can greatly mitigate against the risks and be much more prepared and resilient in the – sadly almost inevitable – event that a breach does occur.

**If you would like to find out more, you can contact Nick Wilding at
nick.wilding@axelos.com**

CONTRIBUTORS' CONTACTS

AlienVault
1875 S Grant Street
Suite 200
San Mateo
CA 94402
USA
Tel: +1 (0) 650 257 8042
Contact: Deepa Chordiya
e-mail: dchordiya@alienvault.com

AXELOS RESILIA
17 Rochester Row
London SW1P 1QT
Tel: +44 (0) 207 960 7865
Contact:Nick Wilding
e-mail: Nick.Wilding@AXELOS.com

Barclays Bank Group Investigations & Insider Threat Programme
Barclays Plc, Level 4
5 The North Colonnade
London E14 4BB
Contact: Christopher Greany
e-mail: Christopher.Greany@barclays.com

BeecherMadden
155 Fenchurch Street
London EC3M 6AL

Tel: +44 (0) 207 382 7980
Contact: Karla Jobling
e-mail: karla.jobling@beechermadden.com

Boolean Logical Ltd
20-22 Wenlock Road
London N1 7GU
El: +44 (0) 780 308 5249
Contact: Nick Ioannou
e-mail: nick@booleanlogical.com

Deutsche Bank AG
Non-Financial Risk Management
Taunusanlage 12
60325 Frankfurt
Germany
Contact: Alexander Ellrodt
e-mail: alexander.ellrodt@db.com

Grant Thornton LLP
30 Finsbury Square
London EC2P 2YU
Tel: +4 (0) 207 383 5100
Contact: Kev Brear
e-mail: Kev.Brear@uk.gt.com

Richard Knowlton Associates Ltd
Office 10096
PO Box 6945
London W1A 6US
Tel: +44 (0) 7500 103164
    +39 3493820008 (Italy)
Contact: Richard Knowlton
e-mail: rk@rkassociates.eu

Layer 8 Ltd
Main House
Colworth Park
Sharnbrook
Bedfordshire MK44 1LQ

Tel: +44 (0) 800 772 0372
Contact: Mike Carter
e-mail: mike.carter@layer8ltd.co.uk
and
Contact: Amanda Price
e-mail: amanda.price@layer8ltd.co.uk

Legend Business Books Ltd
Legend Times Group
107-111 Fleet Street
London EC4A 2AB
Contacts: Tom Chalmers
Direct line: +44 (0) 207 9948
e-mail: tomchalmers@ legend-paperbooks.co.uk
Jonathan Reuvid
Tel: +44 (0) 1295 738070
e-mail: jonathan.reuvid@iprevents.com

Oakas Ltd
Wessex House
Teign Road
Newton Abbot
Devon TQ12 4AA
Tel: +44 (0) 207 127 5312
Contact: Richard Preece
e-mail: richard.preece@oakas.co.uk

PA Consulting Group
10 Bressenden Place
London DW1E 5DN
Tel: +44 (0) 207 881 3519
Contact: Yasmin Greenfield
email: Yasmin.Greenfield@paconsulting.com

Penningtons Manches LLP
125 Wood Street
London EC2V 7AW
Tel:+44 (0) 20 7457 3000
Contact: Dan Hyde
e-mail: dan.hyde@penningtons.co.uk

PGI Group
Cascades 1 1190 Park Avenue
Aztec West
Almondsbury
Bristol BS32 4FP
Tel: +44 (0) 207 887 2699
Contact: Rebecca Preece
e-mail: clientservices@pgitl.com

Proteus-Cyber Ltd
20-22 Wenlock Road
London N1 7GU
Tel: +44 (0) 208 123 7708
Contact: John Clelland
e-mail: john.clelland@proteuscyber.com

Retail Money Market Ltd
55 Bishopsgate
London EC2N 3AS
Tel: +44 (0) 7970 673722
Contact: Dr. Neill Newman
e-mail: security@gnashie.com